Praise for *Shootout*

M000213849

On behalf of my husband I would like to express my deep gratitude for all those responsible for the publication of this book. Cochise County has waited long enough for the truth of this affair. I recognize the tremendous amount of research and work that went into publishing this book, as well as the agonizing of those who were forced to reopen old wounds and relive these tragic events. Jimmy realized that this situation required individuals who were able to think with clarity in difficult circumstances, exercise control, and exhibit compassion, fairness, and the required professionalism. I know that Jimmy V. Judd would be very pleased with the unfailing accuracy of this book—that the truth has at last been exposed. A special thank you to the author, Bill Daniel, and to Larry Dempster for being a man of his word. My heartfelt gratitude goes out to Bert Goodman, Larry Dever (current sheriff), Ray Thatcher, and to all those deputies of Cochise County, and those who helped them ... you were my husband's heroes.

Edna R. Judd

Over time, the "Miracle Valley" event presented probably the most troublesome and challenging circumstances ever to be dealt with by Cochise County Law Enforcement. Many external influences convoluted the entire matter, but through it all two men stood tall—Captain Bert Goodman and Sheriff Jimmy Judd. These men, in their own and distinct ways, helped me understand the meaning of the words bravery, loyalty, and duty. In the words of Charles Dickens, "It was the best of times, it was the worst of times." This book speaks to both.

Larry A. Dever, sheriff of Cochise County

It is my great honor and distinct privilege to recognize one of the greatest sheriffs in Arizona history for the tremendous leadership and professionalism that he exhibited during the near disaster in Miracle Valley, Arizona. In spite of the interference from the highest government officials in our state, Sheriff Judd was able to resolve the Miracle Valley conflict quickly and decisively. Jimmy Judd will always be one of my heroes!

Clarence W. Dupnik, sheriff of Pima County

I met Jimmy Judd when he was chief deputy of Cochise County and later when he became sheriff. It was my privilege and honor to form a close friendship during his tenure. He was a straight up, honorable lawman and a good friend.

After the Miracle Valley incident Jimmy called me to say the governor was getting adversely involved in his actions. Being president of the Arizona Sheriffs and County Attorneys Association, I called a meeting of all sheriffs and county attorneys. We held a meeting in Pima County Sheriff Clarence Dupnik's office. All members of the Association were present.

Out of that meeting, a position paper was drafted which was voted on and passed unanimously by the membership. In essence the paper said that we supported Sheriff Judd's actions and further pledged support for each other in matters of mutual interest in the future.

Immediately following the meeting, I designated Apache County Attorney Steve Udall to read the statement to the media. It was the least we could do for Sheriff Judd.

C. Arthur (Art) Lee, sheriff of Apache County (1973–1998), retired

Over the years many friends have asked me about what happened at Miracle Valley. It was complicated and hard to tell. Now I can say read the book. This book tells what happened and the way it happened.

Captain Bert Goodman, Cochise County Sheriff's Department (retired)

Many of us who were directly involved in the incidents related to the conflicts in Miracle Valley in the early 1980s have been frustrated over the years, in that we have felt the truth of the matter was never really brought to light for the public. We were unable, due to the criminal and civil court actions that were pending, to respond to the outrageous accusations that were made against us in the media by persons who, for the lack of a better term, held or hold to this day "celebrity status." We had hoped that the truth would become known during the trials, but the trials never materialized, denying what we hoped to be our opportunity for justice. I am glad that this book offers some balance to the picture of the events that occurred, why they happened, and will help vindicate those of us that were so vilified in the press. Lives were lost, and all of the lives of those of us who were there were forever altered by these events. To have the truth finally brought to light brings a sense of closure.

Rod Rothrock, chief deputy, Cochise County Sheriff's Department

In the late 1970s no one expected to have southeast Arizona disrupted by a religious cult from Chicago, but it happened. Sheriff Jimmy Judd and the Cochise County Sheriff's Department attempted to keep peace and harmony in the county, but our efforts were hindered by the Arizona governor and the director of the Arizona Department of Public Safety. The death and injuries of the cult members and the deputies are on the hands of political-minded individuals, who told the cult members we were coming in to arrest two men when we thought we were coming in as a surprise. Deputy Jeff Brown, who died from his injuries, Deputy David Jones, shot three times, and my partner Vincente Madrid, with a piece of metal in his arm to this day from his injuries, along with all of us injured who entered the valley that morning should remember Babbitt and Milstead as the cause of those injuries and death. The late Sheriff Jimmy Judd wanted the story told to enlighten the people with what really happened in Miracle Valley. This book is the best avenue for that. Larry Dempster, a longtime friend of Jimmy Judd, put this book on track and got it completed. I thank Larry for having the determination and heart to do that. Also, thanks to Bill Daniel for putting pen to paper and meeting with all of us constantly to get the accurate account of what happened in the early part of the 1980s.

William A. Townsend, Cochise County Sheriff's Department (retired)

This is a story that has long been waiting to be told. This is a story of dedicated Cochise County, Arizona, lawmen and women who were wrongly accused of murder and racism after a gunfight with members of a Chicago-based group known as the Christ Miracle Healing Center and Church.

Others have told the story of the Miracle Valley, Arizona, gunfight, but only from the perspective of politicians trying to gain national political office, lawyers representing the church members, and those members of that church who clashed with the citizens of Miracle Valley and Cochise County law officers. Never before has the story been told by those police officers who were directly involved in the Miracle Valley case.

Now, after all these years, the story is told in the full light of the evidence that was never presented in a court trial. The officers, investigators, intelligence agents, and forensic pathologists—who have lived with the memory of this case for over twenty-seven years—can now tell you *their* story. It is long overdue.

Bill Breen, former Cochise County sheriff's sergeant, former Arizona intelligence agent, and retired Arizona Department of Public Safety detective lieutenant

Shootout at Miracle Valley

Also by William R. Daniel

Radio

West of the Story

Screenplays

Shootout at Miracle Valley
A Short Ride to Paradise
The Ruby Boys
A Cowboy Died Today

Next book

The Memo That Changed the World

Shootout at Miracle Valley

William R. Daniel

Shootout at Miracle Valley

Copyright © 2009 William R. Daniel. All rights reserved. No part of this book may be reproduced or retransmitted in any form or by any means without the written permission of the publisher.

Published by Wheatmark
610 East Delano Street, Suite 104
Tucson, Arizona 85705 U.S.A.
www.wheatmark.com

Cover photo: Cochise County deputy Ray Thatcher retreats as a member of the Christ Miracle Healing Center and Church hurls a rock at him during the shootout at Miracle Valley. Other pursuing women are not shown in the picture. Photo courtesy of the *Arizona Daily Star*.

Back cover photos: Governor Bruce Babbitt, Sheriff Jimmy Judd, and Jesse Jackson. All photos courtesy of the *Arizona Daily Star*.

Publisher's Cataloging-In-Publication Data
(Prepared by The Donohue Group, Inc.)

Daniel, William R. (William Robert)
  Shootout at Miracle Valley / William R. Daniel.
    p. : ill. ; cm.
  Includes bibliographical references.
  ISBN: 978-1-60494-152-4
1. Cochise County (Ariz.)—History—20th century. 2. Miracle Valley
(Ariz.)—History—20th century. 3. Hate—Religious aspects—Christian-
ity. 4. Religious fanaticism—Christianity—Arizona—History. 5. Christ
Miracle Healing Center and Church—History. 6. Miracle Valley (Ariz.)—
Race relations. 7. Cochise County (Ariz.)—Race relations. I. Title.
F817.C5 D26 2008
979.1/53   2008932082

THIS BOOK IS DEDICATED to Sheriff Jimmy Judd, the deputies of Cochise County, and the Judd family. It was the dying wish of Sheriff Judd that the untold story of the Shootout at Miracle Valley be told. Sheriff Judd's longtime friend, Larry Dempster, granted Judd's last wish—to see that the true story was made public and justice was finally given to the men and women who served Cochise County so loyally during the tumultuous period from 1979–1982. These men and women prevented untold deaths by their remarkable restraint and courage. Finally, Sheriff Judd would not think this dedication complete unless it included those individuals in the DPS that served their fellow law enforcement officers so steadfastly—ignoring the political storm that swirled about them.

Contents

Introduction

COCHISE COUNTY, ARIZONA, IS larger than the states of Rhode Island, Delaware, and Connecticut. It is only one hundred square miles smaller than New Jersey. It fills the imaginations of people throughout the world of the Wild West—gunfights, gamblers, and Indian wars. Cochise County was a place where men and women shaped their place in history—the Earps, Clantons, McLaurys, Doc Holliday, Sheriff Behan, John Slaughter, lawman Jeff Milton, Big Nose Kate, and outlaw Burt Alvord.

From Europe to Asia, people are aware of the famous Shootout at the OK Corral, which pitted the Earps and Doc Holiday against the Clantons and McLaurys. The gunfight on the afternoon of October 26, 1881, in Tombstone, Arizona, has entered the folklore of Americana.

Few people are aware that a little over one hundred years later, Cochise County again blazed forth onto the world stage with the same ferocity and publicity that the Shootout at the OK Corral produced. Politicians and power brokers from across the country were momentarily drawn into the spotlight that illuminated the bloody Shootout at Miracle Valley.

Unlike the earlier tragedy at Tombstone's OK Corral, the Shootout at Miracle Valley has been largely ignored, forgotten, and covered up. It is a story that involves bigger than life characters—Sheriff Jimmy Judd, Lawman Bert Goodman, Deputy Ray Thatcher, Jesse Jackson, Bruce Babbitt, Reverend A. A. Allen, and Pastor Frances Thomas. It is a story of bravery, restraint, fear, religious fanaticism, racism, cowardice, and betrayal.

It is a tale that makes people uncomfortable. Voices of fear were raised against the writing of this book as well as a motion picture which is in the works. Some readers of the screenplay and this book ask, "Can't we put this behind us?" "Why do you want to dig this up—hasn't it healed?" "I thought we were past this."

The problem is one can never get past the truth. This story is as old as our country—its lessons as old as civilization. Yet the story of the Shootout at Miracle Valley is as current as today's headlines.

The base instincts for power, control, and dominance are not the sole property of a race, gender, or political group. The uncomfortable truth is racism, hatred, religious fanaticism, and the hunger for power can be exercised by anyone—whites, blacks, and Asians. It can be lodged in the soul of short people, tall people—or ministers who are sometimes from Chicago.

Likewise, the caprice of honor, loyalty, and courage are traits found in the heart. These traits often reside in unlikely hosts. Because of the uncommon nature and exercise of these traits, heroes are often overlooked. We want to stereotype our heroes as well as our villains. The Shootout at Miracle Valley is in the final analysis a story of villains and heroes, ignorance and restraint. It is about people who think they can ignore the truth, without consequence.

Today, many of the participants of the Shootout at Miracle Valley are dead, but others still occupy positions of authority and prominence. As noted before, this book is dedicated to the brave men and women who served Cochise County—Sheriff Jimmy Judd and family and his deputies. Once again, Cochise County shapes history.

Chapter One

In the Beginning

"The worst part of the explosion was having to swallow two mouth-fuls of Brother Stevie."

Female occupant of van[1]

SHE SAT DIRECTLY BEHIND Steve Lindsey when the grey Ford van roared out of Miracle Valley to perform God's work, or rather the work of God's prophet on earth, Pastor Frances Thomas. Frank Bernard piloted the vehicle on its collision course with fate. Behind him a determined Brother Gillespie sat—his eyes forward. In the very back seat there were two additional soldiers of God.

As followers of the transplanted evangelical and racist Pastor Thomas they were bringing God's justice to the infidels—devils, who had unjustly locked up two of their followers in the Cochise County Sheriff's substation in Sierra Vista. As a bonus they might be able to take out the number one devil himself—Sheriff Jimmy Judd.

Steve Lindsey cradled the instrument of their black fury in his lap—an expertly crafted bomb containing enough dynamite to communicate their displeasure. The transplanted sect from the south side of Chicago was not going to tolerate anyone who interfered with their destiny. They were God's fist and their inheritance was to be Cochise County. They would make the Arizona desert bloom in their image, even if they had to blow it up in the process.

With a load of a dozen bombs, handguns, and carbines, who could stand in their way? Behind them a carload of Commandos for Christ sped along with them—God's infantry. The hot Arizona sun beat down on the van, but they didn't notice it. The van speeded up. It was time to arm the bomb. Steve connected the wires to the bomb's battery. And then destiny really stepped in. Perhaps it was his ring or his nerves. Nevertheless, the circuit was completed and unfortunately

1

for the young woman behind him, she was talking when the bomb blew Steve Lindsey to his maker. Her mouth filled with shredded flesh.

It was not the end of the story nor was it the beginning. The story began, as often happens, with someone thinking they were doing a good deed. All of which recalls the old saying, "Beware of what you do in the name of good." Or in this case, in the name of God.

A Miracle in the Desert

The events that led to Steve Lindsey's explosive departure from Arizona history and ultimately to the Shootout at Miracle Valley are complex. They are more complicated and charged than those that resulted in the famous Shootout at the OK Corral. The story finds its roots in the religious fervor of a charismatic man named Asa Alonzo Allen, aka A. A. Allen.

Allen's mother was a full-blood Cherokee who was rumored to like the company of men besides her husband. Allen's father was an alcoholic. At twenty-three, Allen was a man with a drinking problem, looking for salvation. He found it in Miller, Missouri, where two women were preaching at a revival meeting. Allen felt the Holy Spirit and by 1947 he was preaching at a large Assemblies of God Church in Corpus Christi, Texas.

After attending an Oral Roberts tent meeting in 1949, Allen was determined to spread the word nationally. He began to hold "Healing Revival Campaigns." In 1955, he purchased a tent for eighty-seven hundred dollars that could hold ten thousand people. In that same year, Allen was arrested for drunk driving in Knoxville, Tennessee. In reaction to his arrest, the Assemblies of God defrocked Allen. He confronted the unfortunate turn of events by jumping bail. He re-ordained himself and set up the "Miracle Revival Fellowship." In 1958 he bought a tent that could hold twenty thousand sinners.[2] A. A. Allen was on his way to the big time and to Arizona.

As Allen's ministry grew, *Look Magazine* declared him one of the most influential evangelists of the twentieth century. The magazine described Allen as "the nation's topmost tent-toting, old-fashioned evangelical roarer."[3]

Allen was also one of the first modern preachers to mix the

powerful promise of personal prosperity and salvation. He began selling "prosperity cloths" for one hundred and one thousand dollar donations. In the process, Allen grew wealthy and found his own miracle in the desert.

On January 1, 1958, Allen brought the word of God and his twenty thousand-person tent to Phoenix, Arizona, for a winter camp meeting. A typical Allen performance consisted of healing, miracles, hallelujahs, and illusions. A sweating Allen would surreptitiously apply a colorless chemical to his forehead—the perspiration and chemical would produce a visible cross and the crowd would go wild.

It was on that New Year's Day that Allen received his own miracle. God spoke to Urbane Leinendecker. Urbane had driven from Palominas in southern Cochise County to the revival in Phoenix. In the midst of the healing and enthusiasm, the Holy Spirit moved Urbane Leinendecker forward toward the perspiring minister. A. A. Allen was about to receive the gift of twelve hundred and eighty pristine acres in Cochise County, Arizona, from Leinendecker.

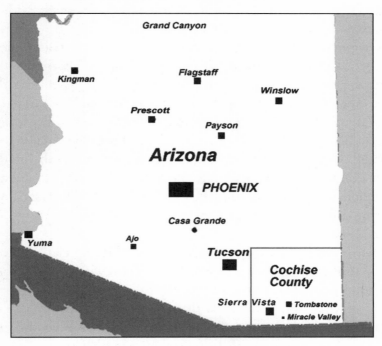

Located in Cochise County, Miracle Valley is
a few miles north of the Mexican border

On January 9, 1958, the deed for the twelve hundred and eighty acres (two square miles) was recorded—deeded to A. A. Allen Revivals, Inc. Allen named the place Miracle Valley.[4]

Raise the Dead

Cochise County was not a stranger to outsiders. People had streamed to the county for one hundred years in search of their dreams. Miners, gamblers, bandits, cattlemen, and merchants came; then more recently hippies came as well. A. A. Allen fit in quite well—and prospered beyond his dreams.

Allen established a Bible college. His campus on the south side of Highway Ninety-two, which bisects Miracle Valley, consisted of several dozen buildings, including a huge domed church (a tabernacle that could house over two thousand worshippers), an enormous warehouse, and an administration building. This ministry was supported by one or two dozen buildings where classes were held and the business of converting the word of God into cash was conducted. Despite his flamboyance, Allen fit into rural Cochise County without a problem. However, his special presence was felt.

On January 1, 1961, a young man from the small Cochise County town of Saint David joined the Cochise County Sheriff's Department as a deputy. Captain Bert Goodman was soon to learn that "A. A. Allen must have thought himself next-to-God."[5]

During a scuffle between some teenagers at a house near Allen's Miracle Valley Bible College, one of the boys was fatally shot. Captain Goodman was investigating the shooting when the mother of the deceased boy appeared. She asked Bert where her son was and Bert replied that he had been taken to a mortuary.[6] She rushed out, blurting that she had to recover the body so the Reverend Allen could bring her boy back to life.

In a similar incident, a young black woman lugging a large suitcase arrived in Benson, Arizona, (a short drive from Miracle Valley) on a Greyhound bus. The sheriff's office was called because of her suspicious behavior—she announced that she needed to see A. A. Allen because her baby had died and she wanted him to resurrect it. Upon opening the suitcase, sheriff deputies discovered her story was true. The dead baby was in the suitcase.

Raise the Cash

Asa Alonzo Allen made few waves. He proceeded to apply his genius for turning faith into cash and was accepted in the sparsely populated county. His sermons were heard nationally on seventy to eighty radio stations (fifty-eight of them daily broadcasts) and forty-three television stations. His *Miracle* magazine went to over three hundred and fifty thousand subscribers and the Bible college received over fifty-five million pieces of mail a year—many of them containing cash. Allen had one hundred and seventy-five employees running the business of religion at the Bible college. His staff was growing.

During these years, Allen's ministry took in over two million dollars annually (which converts to sixteen million dollars in today's world).[7] If this were all Allen did, history would have passed him by without notice. However, Allen ordained ten thousand new faith healers. One of these healers was destined to cast Cochise County onto the national stage—a woman by the name of Frances Thomas.[8]

Endnotes

[1] Interview with Bart Goodwin, September 9, 2008.

[2] www.wikipedia.com

[3] Sacks, Status Report CIV 82-343 TUC_ACM.

[4] www.miraclevalley.net

[5] Interview with Bert Goodman, August 11, 2007.

[6] Interview with Bert Goodman, February 23, 2006.

[7] Sacks, Status Report CIV 82-343 TUC_ACM.

[8] It is interesting to note that on one of Allen's early 1960s recordings of his sermons and services a young Frances Thomas was pictured in the upper right-hand corner of the album cover.

Chapter Two

A True Believer

FRANCES THOMAS WAS BORN in the South and later moved to Illinois. There was nothing exceptional in her childhood. However, in 1957, this changed—and the history of Arizona was to be altered. A. A. Allen brought a month-long tent revival to Cicero, Illinois. Frances Thomas attended every show for the entire month and was overcome by the word of God and Allen's ardent intensity. Frances Thomas later received a "Minister's exhorters card...from Brother Allen."[1] She was aware God was calling her.

When Allen established his Bible college in Miracle Valley, Thomas traveled to Arizona to study the word of God. She was ordained in 1962 and returned to Chicago a dedicated disciple.

Thomas set forth to carry Allen's word to the sinners and convert them to saints. On the fourth Sunday in October 1962, she established the Christ Miracle Healing Church at 58453 Morgan Street in Chicago.[2] Like her mentor, Brother Allen, she was an advocate of faith healing. As proof of her powers, she claimed to have saved a young boy who had swallowed lye and rat poison.

The boy was allegedly taken to the hospital with the lining of his mouth eaten away, and the doctors declared that there was nothing they could do. Pastor Thomas instructed the parents to bring the child home. The pastor held the child through the night and then returned him to his parents. The child was healed—at least according to Thomas.

Spreading the Word

An industrious and energetic Frances Thomas carried her message beyond Chicago to Chocktaw County, Mississippi, and gathered a new group of followers. Her congregation in Mississippi consisted of rural blacks. In general, they were better educated and more prosperous than Thomas's Chicago flock. The Mississippi followers were mostly well mannered and would spend Sunday afternoons at picnics or fishing.

The Chicago church had grown to four or five hundred worshipers. They were tough and streetwise people without much formal education. On hot summer days, they would wait for the white fire department to turn on fire hydrants so they could cool off. They spent their evenings on the stoops and steps of their apartments—angry and looking for salvation. The Chicago church members knew who was to blame for their plight—the white man.

A Dangerous Combination

Frances Thomas's embrace of the fundamental beliefs of A. A. Allen would not in itself be noteworthy—she would have been a footnote in the history of evangelists in twentieth-century America. The problem was Pastor Thomas's beliefs in the word were combined with a virulent hatred toward white people. It was destined to be a potent and deadly cocktail of religion and racism.

Frances Thomas preached holiness, faith healing, and that the coming of the Lord was near. She also fed off the feelings of her Chicago flock that the white man was oppressing black people. She reinforced the idea that *life is terrible at best, and it's never going to get any better—unless you do as Jesus commands, you are doomed to a life of misery on earth and damnation for eternity.*

However, there was good news for the pitiful souls of her congregations. There was a way to happiness and freedom from the white man's unrelenting oppression—and that way was to be illuminated by Frances Thomas. She told her followers that when they heard her speak they were listening to the voice of God. If you were foolish enough not to listen, then damnation was your inheritance.

Thomas's followers were convinced that the whites would never do anything but oppress them. The only way the whites could afford to live in their fancy homes and have black women clean for them was by oppression. Frances and her son, William Thomas, Jr., convinced them that white people's only reason to live was to enslave blacks.[3]

Passion, charisma, and theatrical stunts sold A. A. Allen's message. It may be that Allen was more in love with the profit derived from his mission than the mission itself. Unlike Allen, Frances and William Thomas were true believers—believers who mixed religion and racism with a keen sense of how to make a profit from them.

Endnotes

[1] According to a 1981 radio interview of Pastor Thomas.

[2] There is a conflict in dates regarding Pastor Thomas's ordination by A. A. Allen and her establishment of the Chicago church. In a radio interview she noted that the church was established the fourth Sunday of October 1961. It was also indicated that the church was established after her 1962 ordination.

[3] According to documents recovered by Bill Breen, an investigator and analyst for ACISA (Arizona State Criminal Intelligence Systems Agency).

Chapter Three

The Calm Before the Storm

SIXTEEN YEARS PASSED BETWEEN Frances Thomas's 1962 visit to Cochise County and her next appearance in Arizona. Cochise County was a rural county populated by ranchers, miners, and small-town residents. The biggest cities were Sierra Vista, with the nearby Fort Huachuca military base, and Bisbee, the county seat. In 1970, approximately sixty-two thousand people inhabited the vast county. By the end of the decade, eighty-six thousand people called Cochise County home.

During this period, Bert Goodman's star was on the rise. He became a sergeant, and by 1973 was a captain in the Cochise County Sheriff's Department. In those days, the sheriff's department was responsible for serving warrants, making traffic stops, and investigating burglaries in the rural parts of the county. One of the few incidents to mar an otherwise tranquil period was the day a hippie walked into the Palominas feed store and shot the owner dead during a botched robbery. The hippie took off across country on foot.

The Cochise County Sheriff's mounted unit appeared mostly in parades. However, sometimes a mounted deputy was still useful in apprehending a suspect.

Captain Goodman, who was pulling a horse trailer with his truck that day, and several other deputies pursued the fleeing suspect on horseback as the presumed murderer crossed a ranch south of Palominas. The deputies literally lassoed him and pulled him to the ground. It was at this point that a quality of the sheriff's department presented itself, which was to become even more apparent years later.

The hippie had not only killed a storeowner, but a close friend of the deputies. For a moment, the deputies looked at the hippie and Captain Bert Goodman. There was an unspoken decision to be made: Was there to be frontier justice or the justice of the law? The decision was made: they arrested the hippie. He stood trial and was convicted of murder. Years later, Bert was asked about the incident and why they brought in the hippie. To Bert it wasn't a hard decision: "It was the right thing to do."[1] The moral character demonstrated by Goodman was to be put on display later when the entire sheriff's department was to be tested by Frances Thomas and her fanatical will.

An Offer You Can't Refuse

Another event that occurred in 1973 was to have a more direct influence and importance to the Shootout at Miracle Valley. In 1973, Cochise County Sheriff T. J. "Jim" Willson was looking for a good man to promote.

Captain Bert Goodman

Captain Bert Goodman sat before Cochise County Sheriff Jim Willson.[2] Willson offered Goodman the newly vacated position of undersheriff, a position second only to that of the sheriff in authority. Goodman reluctantly accepted the offer—for a period of a few days.

After reflection, Goodman told Sheriff Willson he wasn't cut out to be stuck under a roof. He respectfully declined to continue as undersheriff. Willson promptly ordered Goodman to find his own replacement.

An Offer That Wasn't Refused

Goodman had just the man for the job—Jimmy Judd. Like Goodman, Judd was from the small Cochise County town of St. David. St. David sits along the San Pedro River, and the area (unlike the rest of the county) is green most of the year because of natural springs.

As a young man, Jimmy excelled at baseball, basketball, and football. He graduated from St. David High School in 1951 and undertook a two-year mission for the Mormon Church. After finishing his mission, he joined the navy for a two-year stint. He returned home, and in 1956 Jimmy married his sweetheart, Edna Tilton.

When Goodman approached Jimmy Judd about the opportunity of becoming undersheriff, his straight-talking friend wasn't convinced. At the age of forty, Jimmy Judd had a family and was doing well as the justice of the peace in Benson. Goodman convinced Judd to talk to Willson.

Other Issues

Jimmy Judd's reluctance to accept the position as undersheriff was not based entirely on his comfort with the position he held as Benson Justice of the Peace. There were some issues with the sheriff's department, and he was well aware of them.

Over a period of time, there had been some trouble with dishonest deputies. Apparently, some deputies were letting prisoners out of jail at night to steal. It was a matter he'd have to handle. Bert Goodman was not the only person pushing for Judd to accept the position of undersheriff. Superior court judges and the county attorney met and wanted someone with an unblemished record to tackle the problems in the sheriff's office. In their mind it was Jimmy Judd.

Judd accepted the job of undersheriff and the challenge to clean up the operation. One of his first acts was to lock down the jail and confiscate over seventy keys from the cells.[2]

Not only did Judd accept the position, but he also ran for sheriff in 1976 and was elected to the first of four terms. Although a contemporary called Judd "one of the last of the true western sheriffs," he also had one foot firmly planted in modern times.[3] Unknown to anyone at the time, Judd was destined for an encounter that had not been seen in Cochise County since the Shootout at the OK Corral.

Endnotes

[1]Interview with Bert Goodman August 11, 2007.

[2]Interview with Judd family August 11, 2007.

[3]According to Pima County Sheriff Clarence Dupnik.

Chapter Four

Welcome to Cochise County!

"The Lord spoke to me and told me to come to Miracle Valley. I don't question God. If he told me go to Africa, I would go to Africa."
Pastor Frances Thomas [1]

IN RESPONSE TO THIS message from God, the Christ Miracle Healing Church in Chicago was put up for sale in 1979. The pastor's son, William Thomas, Jr. and some "saints" from the Chicago church went to Miracle Valley to prepare the way.

Pastor Frances Thomas saw herself as heir apparent to her mentor, A. A. Allen. She dreamed of inheriting the Miracle Valley Bible College that had been established by Allen. Her ambition was to create a religious empire.[2] In 1970, Allen's body was discovered in a room at the Jack Tar Hotel in San Francisco, surrounded by liquor and pill bottles. It was reported (and is denied to this day by supporters of the deceased evangelist) that Allen died of acute alcoholism.[3]

The Bible college had been transferred to a Hispanic Assembly of God group and legally could not be sold for twenty years. In response, Pastor Thomas noted that the end of times was near and believed it was foolish to buy property.

Despite the disappointment and the expected end times, Brother William (as William Thomas, Jr. was called) and Julius "Gus" Gillespie (Pastor Thomas' self-proclaimed "left hand man") came west and scouted Miracle Valley.

The First Wave

Pastor Thomas's son William, Jr. and Julius Gillespie arranged the cash purchase of several acres and numerous buildings in Miracle Valley. In the process they spent over $200,000.[4] Church members began to arrive without fanfare in the fall of 1979. They moved into some modest homes on the north side of Highway Ninety-two. They were the first of many new arrivals that Miracle Valley could expect.

At that time, Miracle Valley was a small community of a hundred or a hundred and fifty residents. They were a mixture of retirees, former followers of A. A. Allen, or people that worked in Sierra Vista, twenty miles to the north. It was a quiet community of whites, Hispanics, and some blacks. Across the highway, the Bible college languished in the dim glow of its bygone glory days.[5]

The first wave of Pastor Thomas's flock that came to Miracle Valley was from Chocktaw County, Mississippi. In general, their neighbors welcomed them. Dorothy Wolfe, an elderly black woman and longtime resident, noted that the established residents "were nice to Christ Miracle Healing Center and Church (CMHCC) people—giving them things like rabbits [and] chickens ..."

William Thomas, Jr. acquired the abandoned Valley View Restaurant located at the corner of Highway Ninety-two and Healing Way to turn it into the new church for the CMHCC. Gil Weatherby, a Miracle Valley resident, "spent seven months and money out of his own pocket remodeling the building for the CMHCC."[6]

Shortly after the first influx of new residents, parents started to enroll their children in the nearby Palominas Elementary School. Gene Brust, school superintendent for the Palominas School District, recalls the parents as, "Nice enough folks who seemed like good parents who only wanted the best for their kids."

Brust remembers the children from Mississippi as well mannered and well educated. They didn't need special attention and earned good grades. The twenty-five Mississippi kids fit into their new school well—they got along with their classmates, on and off the playground.[7]

In another demonstration of local good will, sixth grade teacher Joan Grenough attempted to give an acreage to the Christ Miracle Healing Center and Church. By the time William Thomas, Jr., communicated the offer to his mother in Chicago, it was too late. Grenough donated the property to the struggling Bible college across the highway.[8]

Destiny Calls—Quietly

Cochise County Sheriff's Captain Bert Goodman, Sergeant Don Barnett, Deputies Vince Madrid, Bill Townsend, and Ray Thatcher routinely patrolled the Palominas, Hereford, and Miracle Valley areas. Although they noticed the influx of new faces—especially because there had not been that many blacks in the area in the past, they didn't think much about it.

The officers would wave and when they introduced themselves to the newcomers, they exchanged small talk. The new residents were not too gregarious but seemed like decent people with families.

Sheriff Jimmy Judd became aware of their presence only through casual conversation with his deputies. There was nothing to be alarmed about and no one in the CCSO (Cochise County Sheriff's Office) had heard about Pastor Frances Thomas or the new church.

Even if the sheriff had heard of Pastor Thomas or the new church, it would not have created any concern. There was certainly no indication that the pastor or the church would change the townspeople's destinies. From the time of its discovery by Mormon settlers to A.A. Allen's thriving operation, Cochise County has had a long record of religious tolerance.

Settling In

Like new arrivals anywhere, the newcomers soon discovered where to buy groceries and gas. There was even a small general store with gas pumps right at the corner next to where their new church was being readied—which was essentially the southwest corner of the area soon to come under Mrs. Thomas's control. The small community of Miracle Valley, located three miles north of the United States and Mexican border was growing.

Endnotes

[1] According to a 1981 radio interview with Pastor Thomas.

[2] The Arizona Republic, October 25, 1987.

[3] "Evangelist's Death Due to 'Alcoholism'", Washington Post, June 27, 1970.

[4] The Arizona Republic, October 25, 1987.

[5] It is interesting to note that five years after Allen's death, thirty-two thousand letters a month still arrived at the Bible college addressed to him.

[6] Quote by Weatherby at meeting held by Jesse Jackson in Miracle Valley, November 11, 1982.

[7] Interview with Gene Brust, May 5, 2006.

[8] Interview with Joan Grenough, December 14, 1983.

Chapter Five

Chicago Comes to Cochise County

LATE IN 1979, CHANGES began to appear. The majority of Pastor Thomas's Chicago congregation was arriving in "The Promised Land." Soon, nearly three hundred church members descended on Miracle Valley—a population explosion for the small community. Deputies who normally patrolled the area noted the influx of newcomers but were not alarmed. The officers continued to wave as they passed residents and make small talk when on foot.

Sheriff Judd was informed during regular briefings of the new residents arriving in their jurisdiction. The Sheriff was given general information. At first there didn't appear to be any reason for concern.

Shortly after the dramatic population increase, a new sign appeared in front of the defunct Valley View Restaurant. The remodeled building was identified as "The Christ Miracle Healing Center and Church." It became obvious that the immigration of so many people was the result of an organized effort.

The sign was an indication of the cohesive structure of the new arrivals. When the first wave of immigrants arrived from Mississippi, they did not indicate or mention any affiliation. The Chicago wave made their affiliation to the new church obvious. Although it was a source of interest and conversation in the rural county, there was no concern by the townspeople. The county's long tradition of religious tolerance was ready to embrace another group—in fact, in light of A. A. Allen's old operation across the highway; the establishment of a new church was nothing new and even seemed logical.

Deputy Ray Thatcher would make it a point to stop from time to time somewhere in the neighborhood or the small corner gas station/convenience store. He would run into new residents, introduce himself, and chat.

Something's Changed

Deputy Thatcher was struck by a couple of things that seemed odd. There was a distinct change in attitude and behavior. The first arrivals from Mississippi had appeared open, pleasant, and reasonably friendly. They were well mannered, smiled, and said hello and thank you.

This began to change. Deputies Vince Madrid and Bill Townsend, whose beat also included Miracle Valley, noticed the same thing. It was like a switch had been flipped. Something had definitely changed and it wasn't just with the newer arrivals. Things were different with the other residents as well.

The second thing that Deputy Thatcher and his colleagues noticed was that none of the new arrivals were *ever* alone. Lieutenant Homer Fletcher recalls that the new arrivals became clannish and regularly demonstrated rude behavior. Fletcher noted, "The first group, the ones from Mississippi, didn't behave that way. Not until Mrs. Thomas arrived."[1]

The Second Coming

The late 1979 arrival of Mrs. Thomas in Miracle Valley was a tipping point in the history of Cochise County. Every knowledgeable person interviewed or researched for this book agrees—often with the same words of Homer Fletcher, "The day Mrs. Thomas arrived, everything changed."

Pastor Frances Thomas. Photo courtesy of the Herald Dispatch and Bisbee Review.

One of the white neighbors who had befriended some of the earlier arrivals raised rabbits for food and gave a few to one of the kids. He was excited and grateful. That was before

Mrs. Thomas moved in. Within three days of her arrival, that same nice kid, backed up by several adults, showed up at the white neighbor's door, threw the rabbits into the house, and abruptly announced, "We don't take charity from white men."[2] This was not an isolated incident. Such things quickly became the norm.

White Miracle Valley resident Annett Duran told Sheriff Judd that she had several contacts with teenagers from the church including Darryl Drew, Jerome Pipkins, and Lonnie Hayes. After Mrs. Thomas arrived, these acquaintances became withdrawn and they expressed fear of being caught with white children.

Neighbors began to report to deputies that the newcomers made them nervous. They were standoffish, wore "mean expressions," and made bigoted remarks.[3]

The observation of long time Miracle Valley residents and deputies that something had fundamentally changed was not imagined— nor was it an accident. According to church leader Julius Gillespie, Frances Thomas did not like what she saw when she came to Miracle Valley. She concluded her congregation was too friendly with their white neighbors. She thought it was against God's ordinances…to associate with the people that lived there.

Pastor Thomas took action. She called a meeting of her followers and told them in no uncertain terms that they no longer could associate with the white residents of Miracle Valley.[4]

Mission Statement

Mrs. Thomas was very forthcoming about informing her neighbors that, "She had been called by God to take over Miracle Valley." The old residents—many of whom had lived there for decades— weren't interested in seeing Mrs. Thomas or anyone else take over their valley. As they would soon learn, she was in deadly earnest. She was determined to have Miracle Valley by any means necessary.[5]

The first news around the sheriff's department of concern about the group, according to Deputy Vince Madrid, had to do with traffic stops by the Sierra Vista Police Department. "We weren't involved in anything yet and it was more scuttlebutt than intelligence. We were also hearing rumbles that it was an organized church group, but that alone was certainly nothing to worry about," Madrid said.

Sergeant Don Barnett, the sheriff department's primary man in Miracle Valley, noted the obvious change in the church members' attitudes. The tough, no-nonsense Barnett sat down with Sheriff Judd and told him, "Something is *not* right in Miracle Valley."

At this point, in the fall of 1979, there was no evidence of any wrongdoing. A few grumbles from neighbors who were confused about the new arrival's behavior along with similar reports from the deputies did not constitute a call for action.

Since at that point there was no real cause for alarm, Sheriff Judd ordered his deputies to simply keep an eye on things in Miracle Valley and see to it that he and Sergeant Barnett were informed of anything noteworthy.

Endnotes

[1] Interview with Homer Fletcher, March 8, 2006.

[2] Interview with Homer Fletcher, March 8, 2006.

[3] Interview with Ray Thatcher, March 8, 2006.

[4] Arizona Republic, October 25, 1987.

[5] It is worth noting that according to a taped interview with Sheriff Judd, Pastor Thomas later told him that she wanted to control Cochise County.

Chapter Six

Palominas School

LATE IN THE FALL of 1979, parents and guardians—often a child's aunt who was referred to as *Auntie*—brought their children to the nearby Palominas School for enrollment. The number of school-aged children from the Mississippi arrivals enrolled in Palominas School was a little over two dozen.[1] The second wave of newcomers from Chicago tripled the number of new pupils. It became evident almost immediately that the new pupils bore little resemblance to the kids from Mississippi.

The Mississippi children were as well educated as their peers. They did not require remedial education to catch up to the other children. The Mississippi students had also proven to be well mannered and fit in well with the rest of the students.

The Chicago children were the opposite. School Superintendent Gene Brust recalls them as "being very poorly educated and equally ill mannered. They were clearly way behind our student body, and that includes the first group of children from the church."

Meeting the Challenge

It became clear the new children could not properly deal with their normal course load. While they were able to attend some of the regular classes, the school had no option but to create special classes to help them reach the educational level of the other students. But even in these special classes, the attitude was not only one of disinterest, but the students often behaved belligerently toward their teacher.

Many teachers worked beyond normal school hours to help the students. Teacher Joan Grenough tells of "teachers staying for an hour after school" to help tutor the children who were struggling to keep up in school.[2] Grenough tried to encourage them with hugs when they did well, but to no avail. The influence of Pastor Thomas was too pervasive. Pastor Thomas instilled and nurtured a spirit of mistrust and belligerence in the children.

Disturbing Signs

It was almost of equal concern that the children often appeared semi-comatose. It was as if they had not slept for days. They were becoming dull and unresponsive. It seemed that some of their behavior and hostility issues were the result of exhaustion.

"They were like zombies," said Gene Brust. "And another thing that was really bothering us all was that the kids from Mississippi, the first ones who were doing so well and fitting in, were back-sliding. Their grades were slipping and their behavior was degenerating. They were becoming just like the others."

The new students were also very standoffish—staying together and avoiding contact with children that did not belong to the Christ Miracle Healing Center and Church. It also was becoming clear this isolationist behavior was splitting the school along racial lines. It now had little to do with whether the students were new or old and had everything to do with the color of their skin.

The black students shunned the white kids, many who had made overtures of friendship, with indifference or rudeness—a rudeness that reflected a growing racial mistrust. Brust and the teachers watched the widening rift. It appeared to them that newcomers were living in an environment of racial mistrust and paranoia. The new students certainly did not develop these attitudes unaided. Their clannishness and shunning of white students was not spontaneous or accidental.

The new students never allowed themselves to be alone, and were always in the company of the largest possible group of their church peers. Their behavior became cause for serious concern. The school had hundreds of other students who couldn't comprehend the change and were becoming frightened of the newcomers who clearly didn't like them.

Brainwashing and Indoctrination

It was also obvious that the newcomers had been taught that whites were the enemy—student or teacher alike—and were to be dealt with or tolerated only as necessary. The fact that the black students had been carefully schooled in that attitude became even clearer the day a teacher arrived at Brust's office with a full-color comic book she had found in her classroom.

The subject matter was chilling. It was a treatise of racial hatred. On every page, whites screamed violent epithets at guiltless blacks, calling them niggers as they beat and stabbed them—knives dripping with black blood. The discovery of the comic book solidified the staff's understanding of the origins of the transformation that the children's attitudes had undergone.

The children's behavior on the playground was another clear demonstration of their training. They stayed together and completely avoided white students whenever possible. When they were forced to have contact with white students, they were not only rude, but often violent.

The violence typically only amounted to pushing and shoving, but was still completely unacceptable. A teacher would intervene, of course. Such was the job of the playground monitor. But quietly explaining the situation to reasonable children never happened. The church children greeted the teacher's intervention like they dealt with all other white contact.

The newcomers viewed the teacher's intrusion as racial aggression. According to the church students, the teacher wasn't stopping unacceptable behavior—they were attacking blacks. It was the only response the new students knew. A teacher would instantly be surrounded by a dozen black students, called names, and threatened with menacing gestures.

It was no longer just the white kids who felt threatened; the teachers now shared the children's fear. Superintendent Brust and the teachers at Palominas School were firmly convinced: the church was running a school of its own. It was a school of bigotry and hatred and the children were obviously getting excellent grades.

An Ugly Turn

Not only were the new children undergoing a careful program of training in hatred, but also the first sign of physical abuse appeared. Mrs. Grenough, who taught sixth grade, gave Monica Rushing all C's on her report card. The result was swift and harsh. Monica came to school with her hands swollen—she had been beaten because her grades were poor.

Joan Grenough went to the school principal and received permission to give sixth-grader Monica Rushing all A's in the future, but with an asterisk next to those grades indicating they were for performance at a third-grade level! The result was no more swollen fingers.[3]

Endnotes

[1] Interview with Gene Brust, May 5, 2006.

[2] Page 24 of Grenough sworn interview on December 18, 1983.

[3] Grenough sworn interview on December 18, 1983.

Chapter Seven
A Modern Sheriff

SHERIFF JIMMY JUDD WAS not only "one of the last of the true western sheriffs," he was also the first modern Sheriff of Cochise County. His experience as justice of the peace in Benson had taught him the value of being organized, managing situations, and understanding people. Although he had a reputation as a straight talker, he was also an agent of change. People that knew him recall him as a kind man whose word was his bond. When these characteristics were merged with his sense of justice, he was a formidable force.

Jimmy Judd was more than one of the last true western sheriffs

Judd started the process of moving the Cochise County Sheriff's Department into the twentieth century. Before Pastor Thomas arrived in Cochise County with her flock, Judd was busy transforming the department from "a good old boy" system toward one of increased professionalism.[1] Judd required regular training for deputies and organized the system of promotions. He also promoted equal pay for men and women in the department.[2] One other characteristic that typified Sheriff Jimmy Judd was patience—and that was the characteristic that Pastor Frances Thomas was to test to its limits.

Patience and Patrols

The events at the school were troubling. Events in Miracle Valley were also becoming more serious. Old-time residents were becoming increasingly nervous. Their new neighbors were beginning to reflect the same attitude that had become prevalent at Palominas School.

Sheriff Jimmy Judd sensed that there was definitely a cause for concern, and this cause was sufficient enough for him to order his deputies to heighten patrols through the area. The deputies had orders to try to get to know the residents, to see if there were ways to promote goodwill and to keep tensions from escalating.

Deputies Ray Thatcher, Vince Madrid, and Bill Townsend began foot patrols through the area. Their presence was coolly tolerated. Thatcher would initiate conversations with church members. He was even asked by several men if he would teach them to shoot. He said he'd be happy to, even though the request set off a small alarm in Thatcher's head. He wasn't going to go out of his way to pursue this.

Thatcher's earlier observation of church members never being alone in public was verified. The men were always in groups of at least three or four. Women were similarly grouped, as were the children. When a car left Miracle Valley, there were rarely fewer than three men inside, and very few cars ever left unaccompanied by at least two or three vehicles.

Routine Traffic Stops?

The frequency of traffic stops along Highway Ninety-two were increasing and becoming very unpleasant for DPS (Department of Public Safety) officers as well as Cochise County sheriff's deputies. It was common practice for church members, which meant church men—since the women rarely drove—to speed well beyond the fifty-five mile per hour limit and to increase that to whatever speed was necessary in attempt to evade pursuit.

Whenever possible, it became standard procedure for a speeding car to stay ahead of the pursuing law enforcement vehicle until it was able to make it to the church-compound area. There the officer or deputy would be greeted by a large group of angry people, sometimes armed with guns, but almost always with some type of weapon—including rebar, rakes, shovels, and ax handles. The officers were also met with loud racial epithets.

It was clear by now that Pastor Thomas's followers truly believed that any complaint against them was motivated by a deep-seated, unavoidable hatred that all whites held for all blacks. It became equally common for DPS officers and sheriff's deputies to break off pursuit rather than follow a speeder into the CMHCC compound, due to the consequences that would inevitably bring—including the possibility for violence.

It was becoming more than a test of patience. Sheriff Judd was determined not to have a deputy or civilian killed over a traffic violation. "If you can affect that arrest, get it done," he told reporters in defense of his deputies. "But, by damn, if you're going to get killed, get the hell out of there, come back later."[3]

Ominous Events—Bad Neighbors

Encounters between church members and their neighbors (old time whites and blacks) became more frequent. Coy Meeks, one of the white neighbors and a long-time resident of the area, complained to deputies of church members: "They are driving through the area at all hours of the night, yelling and honking horns." While their purpose was not stated, this was obviously intended to harass their neighbors—neighbors who couldn't help but recall Mrs. Thomas's statements about God wanting her to "take over Miracle Valley."

More than anything, Sheriff Judd wanted his deputies to help keep things quiet; not turn a potentially serious situation into a tragic one. No one wanted to read any handwriting on the walls, but the potential within current events was ominous.

Ominous Events—School Situation

Things had also gone downhill at the school. Gent Brust was keeping a close eye on the playground. His teachers were in jeopardy.

"Take over Miracle Valley"

Pastor Thomas's private utterances were often at odds with her public pronouncements. She presented herself to the media as a simple pastor who was merely trying to teach her flock "holiness."

Sheriff Judd later on had several one-on-one encounters with the CMHCC leader (see Chapter Eight) that presented her intentions in a much more direct manner. The Sheriff had a conversation with her about the longtime Miracle Valley residents claim that she wanted to take over Miracle Valley.

The Pastor indicated that her ambitions were much more grandiose. She told the Sheriff she "wanted to take over Cochise County." This surprised Judd. He again asked her what she wanted. The pastor replied, "I want you dead."

Sheriff Judd left the meeting thinking, "That doesn't leave much room for negotiations."[4]

He was the boss and he intended to take charge when necessary. It didn't take long for it to become necessary. One day, a teacher was surrounded. Church children were threatening her and accusing her of being a racist. Brust came out and ordered them to stop. They did, but not without a few of the same verbal slaps aimed at him.

The following day, five men from the church visited the school superintendent. They demanded, in no uncertain terms, a presence on the school playground. Brust permitted them to make their demands. The men were firmly convinced their children were the subject of continual racial attacks and couldn't be properly protected, except by the presence of church members on school property who would maintain a vigil.

The parents also complained about treatment that they alleged their children received on the school bus—they claimed that white children were every bit as abusive on the bus as they were in the schoolyard. Brust's visitors from Miracle Valley now demanded a presence not only in the schoolyard but also on the school buses.

After a moment of silence, Brust told them, "Absolutely NOT!" The men were not pleased, rebutted, "This is not over," and stalked out of the office.

The following day the five men returned. They had accepted, but not happily, Brust's denial of their presence on the school playground. This time, they again insisted that adult church members be allowed to ride the school bus because it was the only way to protect their children.

Again, Brust denied their demand, every bit as forcefully as he had the previous day. And again they let him know in terms just as powerful, "This is still not over."

And it wasn't. The next day, accepting the last two denials and still not at all pleased, the men appeared again. Whether the superintendent liked it or not, the men's children needed to be protected. They presented what they considered was a reasonable compromise that would satisfy both sides: they proposed that cars from Miracle Valley would follow the school buses to and from school.

In addition, the parents would set up an observation post in the school's front parking lot where they could observe and monitor the school yard, if not the interior of the building.

Superintendent Brust's patience had worn thin. "Let me explain this in the simplest terms I can. I can not control what you do in your private cars on a public road. But I can guarantee you, if you interfere with one of our busses at any time in any way, I will have you all arrested. You will not set up in our parking lot. Not for a day. Not for a minute. And if you do, I will have you arrested immediately. I do not want problems with you, but we are in control of our school, not you; and if you force my hand, if you interfere with our operation in any way, I have told you what will happen. I will have you arrested without hesitation."[5]

It was time for increased vigilance. Superintendent Brust related to Sheriff Judd what was happening at the school. In response, Sheriff Judd ordered deputies to begin keeping a closer eye on the school. From then on, they did just that. At least one deputy was stationed across the road from Palominas School every day—and created an obvious presence.

Endnotes

[1] Judy Gignac, a former member of the Arizona Board of Regents who was serving as Cochise County Supervisor at the time of the shootout.

[2] Interview with Edna Judd, August 23, 2008.

[3] Page 83, *Arizona, No Ordinary Journey* by Mary Jo Churchwell.

[4] According to Larry Dempster, Bert Goodman and Judd family.

[5] Interview with Gene Brust, May 5, 2006.

Chapter Eight

A Visit to the Church

WITH REPORTS COMING IN from deputies and now from School Superintendent Gene Brust, Sheriff Judd, wanting more than anything to protect the peace for all of the white and black residents of the area, made the only reasonable decision. It was time to personally meet the members of the Christ Miracle Healing Center and Church on their own turf. He would take only a couple of his most involved men (to minimize any possibility of intimidation) and pay the church a visit.

It was late afternoon near the end of 1979 when Sheriff Jimmy Judd, Undersheriff Dale Lehman and Deputy Ray Thatcher arrived at the church. There were several well-dressed men stationed outside the church. When the sheriff's car pulled up and parked, one of the men disappeared inside the building, obviously to report their arrival.

As Sheriff Judd and his men exited the car, they heard singing from inside, which was hardly unusual for a church service. The churchmen at the door gave the law enforcement officers a cool reception, according to Deputy Thatcher. They were asked their purpose in being there. The sheriff responded that they wanted to introduce themselves and give the church members a proper welcome. While waiting, the sheriff could gaze at the parking area (near the corner of Healing Way and Highway Ninety-two) where so many car chases had ended unpleasantly.

The Word and the Way

When the churchman who had gone in to report emerged after only a few moments, the sheriff and his men were admitted into the building. At the east end of the large room was a riser with a podium on it. Standing at the podium was Pastor Frances Thomas. She was an imposing figure and a powerful speaker. Behind her, where one

36

might expect to see a cross or a picture of Jesus, were two *very* large pictures—one of Pastor Thomas and the other of A. A. Allen.

Before the riser were dozens of folding chairs, separated by a center aisle and space down the sides. The seats were filled with worshippers—at least one hundred and fifty strong—adults and children dressed better than they ever were for school. The service was obviously in progress. Pastor Frances Thomas glanced at her visitors from the altar. The sheriff and his two men stood near the west wall of the sanctuary, holding their hats out of respect.

The officers had no way of knowing

Pastor Frances Thomas was a powerful speaker. She believed God spoke through her. Photo courtesy of the Arizona Daily Star.

that a service was almost always in progress. The congregation was just finishing a hymn. At first, it appeared to Judd and his men to resemble what one would expect to find at any Christian service. Pastor Thomas read from scripture and spoke of devotion to God.

Attention!

As the lawmen quietly observed, they began to notice things that were not so typical of any Christian service they had ever attended. Most notably, a few men and women quietly walked about the room, carefully watching the congregation. While their purpose was not clear, they certainly had the appearance of guards and the long sticks they carried were mysterious.

Children of all ages comprised about one quarter to one third of the worshippers. They were clean and dressed appropriately for church. They were quiet, as one would expect in such an environment. But as the officers observed, something about the children seemed odd. It soon became clear what they were observing. It was precisely the condition reported to them by School Superintendent Gene Brust.

The children weren't simply being quiet. They looked like zombies. They had the exhausted appearance one would expect to see in sleep-deprived people; an observation that would soon be proved accurate. They watched one of the roaming churchmen move silently down an aisle. The man stopped at the end of a row. The purpose of the long sticks became crystal clear. A child had dozed off—his head drooping forward. With the ease and accuracy of a fly-fisherman, the monitor leaned in and whacked the sleeping boy.

The child instantly came awake but he didn't snap to attention as one might expect. He didn't cry or react in any way, other than waking up. He didn't even look over at the man who had struck him. He simply woke up and began paying attention to the service. He not only looked like a zombie—he behaved like one. The effect on the children around him was similar. They straightened in their seats and seemed to become more attentive, but no less zombie-like than the child who been struck.

The Sheriff and his men remained silent and continued to observe. Before the service ended, several more children dozed off and were similarly awakened. The guards made no attempt to hide what they were doing.

No adult (some of whom had to be parents) reacted to their children being struck by the guards. It was quite obviously a common and accepted practice.

The Word of God

When the service ended, Judd, Lehman, and Thatcher walked outside and waited. They spoke with Pastor Thomas, her son William Thomas, Jr., and a group of churchmen and women.[1] They were all similarly well-dressed. The sheriff introduced himself and his men. He let them know that they should feel free to call upon his department at any time and for any reason. He emphasized that they were there to serve the community of which the church and its members were now a part.

A church member asked Sheriff Judd if he could teach them to shoot. Judd responded that they would have to ask Deputy Thatcher, because he was the arms expert. Thatcher smiled. The request was never pursued after that meeting.[2]

Beyond that request, the church members responded that they were quite self-sufficient. They added if the need ever arose they knew how to get in touch. The meeting was cordial if not friendly. None of the church members, including Pastor Thomas, ever smiled.

The sheriff didn't ask about the somnambulistic children or the men who patrolled the room with sticks, nor did he inquire about the strange statements made by Mrs. Thomas near the end of the service. What she'd said was sobering and very *telling*. She reminded her flock that the words that flowed from her mouth were the words of God, and, by clear and obvious implication, that was precisely who she was.

Sgt. Barnett's statement of a few months earlier echoed in the sheriff's head as he walked to his car: "Something was clearly wrong in Miracle Valley."

It should be noted that Linda Sharron, a student at the Southern Arizona Bible College (on the old A. A. Allen property), located across Highway Ninety-two from the Healing Center compound, told the sheriff that while attending services at the CMHCC she observed a black woman hitting children with a stick during the service. Sharron was so upset by what she saw that she decided to leave. She was stopped and warned by Mrs. Thomas that it would not have been a good idea to leave at that time.

Endnotes

[1] Pastor Thomas's son William Thomas, Jr., was known as Brother Thomas. As his power and influence grew within the cult he became known as Bishop Thomas. By the time of the shootout he was also called Field Marshal.

[2] Interview with Ray Thatcher, August 7, 2008.

Chapter Nine

The Cult

PASTOR THOMAS HAD BROUGHT together an impoverished group of poorly educated, angry people who felt excluded from a system they couldn't understand or influence. They were vulnerable and longed for hope and an escape from their predicament.

Asa Alonzo Allen had obvious shortcomings, but his organization was open to people of all races. The cynic might argue that Allen was an equal-opportunity con man, but nonetheless he was preaching a powerful message to the disenfranchised.

Allen proclaimed in his *Miracle* magazine that "when hearts are hungry and God is moving, there is no time for color lines." By the early 1960s, blacks were included in the inner circle of Allen's movement.[1]

A Racial Divide

It appears that Frances Thomas took the theological part of Allen's beliefs to heart, but disregarded the racial inclusiveness that her mentor championed. She married the powerful religious dictums of Allen and cult leaders like Jim Jones (the ideas are that God heals and speaks through chosen people, that true believers should grant their worldly possessions willingly to their spiritual leaders, and that one should never question the authority of these leaders) with the potent power of racism.

To further her power and control, Thomas nurtured the belief that the white race was evil. She created a common enemy whom black people could blame for their situation, and thus gave ample reasons for the black people to hate the white community. She cemented it all together with a God who instructs the church members in anger and paranoia.

Psychologist Dr. Margaret Singer wrote that cult behavior is about the practice and conduct of the group, not its beliefs. Human beings don't do well in a vacuum. We need people. We need to talk about things. We need to argue about things. We need to feel part of something. Without validating human contact, one quickly loses any sense of self-worth. If we live a life of poverty over which we have little control, we can justify being angry with anyone.

Cult mentality is based on making a convincing case to a group eager to find acceptance anywhere. It is what Charles Manson (whose followers believed he was Jesus and gleefully murdered at his behest) did in California. It is what Jim Jones did to his followers because he convinced them it was part of God's great plan.

And convincing her people that her word was part of God's great plan is precisely what Pastor Frances Thomas did in Miracle Valley.

Pastor Frances Thomas and Jim Jones

Jim Jones is remembered as the fanatical leader of the People's Temple. In 1977, he took his followers from the United States to Guyana and created his own enclave called Jonestown. In November 1978, U.S. Congressman Leo Ryan led a fact-finding mission to Jonestown amid allegations of abuse. When Ryan and his party were at an airstrip preparing to leave, gunmen sent by Jones attacked them. Ryan and five others were killed. On November 18, 1978, over nine-hundred Temple members died in Jonestown, all but two from drinking Kool Aid laced with cyanide.

On more than one occasion Pastor Thomas spoke of her contemporary Jim Jones. In times of stress she would invoke his name and threaten "another Jonestown" or say, "If you thought Jonestown was a picnic, you haven't seen anything yet." [2]

During a meeting with Sheriff Jimmy Judd, Thomas asked, "Do you know about Jim Jones and his Kool Aid?" Judd replied, "Yes, ma'am. I've heard about that." She then said, "We already have the punch made." [3]

The sympathies of Thomas obviously were with the man that masterminded the suicide of nine hundred of his flock. Thomas said, "It would have never happened if he had been left alone." [4]

Mind Control 101

By Dr. Singer's reasoning, The Christ Miracle Healing Center and Church was most assuredly a cult. God is a powerful tool and Pastor Thomas was a master craftsman. Thomas was a persuasive speaker with a willing audience. She convinced her flock that she was in direct contact with God and implied with great success that she was, in fact, God (or more specifically, Jesus incarnate.) With that belief firmly implanted, she and her son Bishop William Thomas, Jr., an equally convincing speaker, were able to utilize time-honored mind control techniques.

She had these skills mastered and used them to full advantage.

» *Group acceptance.* This is one of the first and most important aspects of controlling the will of the cult as a whole. There is no denying the Miracle Valley cult was a cohesive body. Every member was continually reinforced in his or her value to the group.

» *Eradication of the individual.* This is another critical element in the equation and was accomplished by the group members' devotion to their God above themselves—which reinforced group acceptance and the unimpeachable premise that their individual value was directly tied to the welfare of the group. William Thomas, Jr. constantly preached of his willingness to be martyred at the hand of law enforcement, because protecting the flock trumped even the value of his own life. He declared, "I am a commando for Christ. I am prepared to give my life. Death plays a sweeter tune than the cold, iron chains of slavery."

» *Us vs. Them.* This was the easiest concept of all for the Pastor. Her hatred for all whites whom she deemed racists was the foundation of her control—a cornerstone she firmly established back in Chicago.

Who has the all money and who lives on welfare? Who has all the power and who has none? Who lives in fine houses eating fine food and who lives in hovels subsisting on food stamps? And who comes with nightsticks and guns and who gets beaten and shot?

Black people were poor and powerless, dependent on the white man's charity, hating him for it, and despising all whites as the reason for their pitiful plight. The white man and his laws designed specifically to keep the black man from achieving anything beyond abject poverty provided an available and readily observable common enemy for Thomas's followers. This was a common enemy she could easily describe with eloquence, because to the deepest recesses of her mind and in the very depth of her soul, this was what she truly believed.

» *Intimidation*. What could possibly be more intimidating than listening to the voice of God? This was a God who rescued black people from dreadful circumstances, brought them together in "Her" name, and provided for them. They believed absolutely in the divinity of their leader and whatever she told them was God's divine law. Thomas not only preached the word, but also healed the sick—and if the sick were to succumb, it was simply God's will.

Her control was absolute. During one of Frances Thomas's healing services, she healed many church members of eye problems. Members were of course not healed, but were so intimidated that they refused to wear their glasses for fear that the others would believe they were not holy enough to have been healed.

Another example of Pastor Thomas' effort to exert complete control over her flock was her practice of arranging marriages between church members.[5]

» *Sleep deprivation*. The more alert one is, the more likely he is to question. Nonstop church services and prayer meetings went a long way in accomplishing the goal of a non-questioning follower. The demand for constant prayer in the home completed the task. Sleep was a rare commodity among CMHCC members in Miracle Valley.

Numerous employers made statements to the sheriff's department that church members, even those who at first seemed alert and interested in their jobs, soon became unable to perform their tasks and appeared too exhausted to function properly. They often became irritable and uncooperative. Virtually every church member who secured employment was eventually fired for incompetence and or uncooperative behavior—or they simply stopped showing up for work.

The effects of sleep deprivation were even more evident in the children.[6] Church services and religion classes were nonstop, often continuing throughout the night. Superintendent Gene Brust said the children "looked like zombies."

As noted earlier, outsiders who attended a church service, as well as deputies would testify that they observed children being whacked awake with long sticks during church services.

Mrs. Thomas was good at what she did. She and her son knew all the tricks and employed them with impunity. The techniques of group acceptance, eradication of the individual, intimidation, and sleep deprivation were combined with their virulent hate of white people—a common enemy with whom they all had a history, and an enemy who was very easy to spot.

Endnotes

[1] *White Sects and Black Men in the South* by David Edwin Harell.

[2] Deposition of Robert Conley, December 6, 1983.

[3] Interview with Edna Judd on August 23, 2008

[4] 1981 Radio Interview with Pastor Thomas.

[5] The Arizona Republic, October 25, 1987.

[6] Deputy Ray Thatcher, who often patrolled Miracle Valley at night, recalled the following in a March 8, 2008 interview. He said he "would pull into the Christ Miracle Healing Center and Church parking lot in the middle of the night—two or three o'clock AM—and listen to the children in the church continuously chanting."

Chapter Ten

The Patrols

DURING A 1981 RADIO interview, Sheriff Judd was asked when he thought the tensions in Miracle Valley started to escalate. The sheriff said the turning point was when the CMHCC started their security patrols in Miracle Valley and along Highway Ninety-two. Little did the sheriff realize that the culmination of those tensions would result in the shootout one year later.

Escalation

Neighbors were reporting increased incidents of harassment by members of the church. Church members were driving through the area at all hours of the night, yelling and honking horns. Sometimes they would station people in shifts around a particular house to intimidate the occupants. More than once, a long-time resident gave into the intimidation and sold his home—to Pastor Thomas.

Deputy Ray Thatcher often patrolled Miracle Valley at night. What he reported was disturbing. One elderly white man had befriended the church members—and for some reason they took it wrong. In the middle of the night people would toss large rocks into the residence. According to Thatcher, "The home he had put all of his life savings into was trashed."[1] Thatcher reported this and other similar incidents to the Sheriff constantly.

The problem was that every time Thatcher patrolled the area, the roving groups were nowhere to be seen. They appeared to have a warning system telling when police were in the area.[2]

Just as alarming were neighbors' reports of being followed by cars full of churchmen. And a new word emerged in the neighbors' complaints: the word was "weapons." Area residents who were fully prepared to testify at the request of the sheriff or prosecutors conveyed the following stories:

Mr. and Mrs. Frank Sennett, retired residents of Miracle Valley:

When members of the CMHCC arrived in Miracle Valley, the Sennetts were living across the street and just east of the Julius Gillespie residence. Sennett noticed two male subjects on guard at all times of the day and night at the Gillespie residence. Often men would leave the Gillespie's house with weapons. They would walk over next to the Sennett's property and begin randomly firing large handguns. Sennett requested they stop shooting near his residence. One church member laughed at him, made an obscene gesture, and continued shooting.

Church members would drive through the neighborhood throughout the day and night, blowing their automobile horns and shinning lights into yards.

(Shortly thereafter, the Sennetts left Miracle Valley and moved to Sierra Vista.)

Jim Melton, Miracle Valley Resident:

After the arrival of Pastor Thomas, Melton noticed a change in the attitudes of the CMHCC members. Church members would drive by his home, stop, and state, "We claim this property in the name of the Lord." The members would also throw rocks at his vehicle.

In addition to witnessing CMHCC members harass the sheriff's deputies; he saw they began to carry weapons.

May Belle Taylor, a black resident of Miracle Valley:

Taylor, an ordained minister, did not escape abuse. The twenty-year resident of Miracle Valley was routinely intimidated by CMHCC members. She was told she was no good because she associated with white people.

White residents in their cars were now being regularly followed through the area by carloads of black men who were tailgating and honking horns. Weapons were almost always apparent.

Pastor Thomas had never been shy about telling people that God wanted her to take over Miracle Valley. All evidence pointed to her trying to do just that by using intimidating tactics to drive out the existing residents.

Equal Opportunity Harassment

As noted with May Belle Taylor's experience, Pastor Frances Thomas's followers sometimes directed their wrath at black people. The justification for their harassment of Mrs. Taylor was her friendships with whites.

The justification for harassing another black woman must have risen from their paranoia about outsiders. A leading member of the NAACP (Los Angeles Chapter) had been visiting relatives in Sierra Vista. She decided to take a ride with her granddaughter. They made the mistake of stopping at the CMHCC service station at the corner of Highway 92 and Healing Way to use the bathroom.

When told that the service station didn't have a bathroom, they went next door to Pastor Thomas's church. Instead of her granddaughter being able to use the toilet, they were chased out, and retreated to their car—followed closely by an angry group of church members throwing rocks and cans. Another relative was sitting in the rear seat of the car with the window down. As the unwelcome visitors drove away, the woman in the rear seat was struck by a rock and suffered a broken arm. After receiving medical treatment the victims contacted Sheriff Judd and County Attorney Beverly Jenny and reported what happened. Shortly after this instance, such attacks were to become better organized.

A Mysterious Crime

In February of 1980, someone broke into a house occupied by church members John and Willie Mae Drew. They were absent at the time. No one was injured and nothing of any significance was taken. The Drews reported the incident to the sheriff's department. When the deputies responded and examined the property, no evidence of any kind was discovered. The Drews could offer nothing to aid in the investigation except, of course, their supposition that the intruders must have been white—probably one of the nearby residents who despised them.

It was that incident that stimulated Mrs. Thomas and her son, the church's recognized "field marshal," into creating a systematic network of security patrols. This amounted to cars with two to four armed churchmen who cruised the area looking for trouble.

When questioned about the practice by deputies who were receiving complaints from longtime residents, the church members responded by claiming the sheriff's department wasn't protecting them; they were only helping the white residents. The congregation asserted that the whites constantly harassed them and that the department was only responding to the white residents' complaints. The church members insisted that if they didn't do something to protect themselves no one would.

Organizing the Security Patrols

Non-church residents of the area regularly witnessed churchmen in martial-arts training and practicing with firearms.

Lieutenant Frank Peterson met with church members, who asked if they could organize neighborhood watches. He acknowledged that as long as they followed certain rules, there was nothing wrong with the watches. The church members believed he granted them tacit approval for their patrols. It was then that the patrols began in earnest.

The hierarchy of the church organized and embraced the new patrol with ease. The command structure flowed down from Pastor Thomas to William Thomas, Jr., who was the field marshal. His second-in-command was a man named Ray Charles Carter. Thomas, Jr. called the members of the patrol "Commandos for Christ."

The security patrol was organized into four flights. Flight A was commanded by Lieutenant Dorothy Williams and consisted of women. The other three Flights (B, C, and D) were commanded by Lieutenant Frank Bernard, Lieutenant Sherman McCain, and Lieutenant Billy Bernard. Below these commanders were sergeants. Each flight was given a different shift.

The church's security force communicated with radios and developed a code to disguise their activities from unwelcome eavesdroppers. Below are several security patrol members and their "handles":

| Brother William | Chi-Kon | 032 |
| Brother Amos | Ki Sunn | 029 |

Brother Brutus	Ki-Tan	019
Brother Terry Tate	Tempo	021
Brother Ray Carter	Kun-Tai	027
Sister Dorothy	Sharkiss	025
Sister Mary	Sun-Dust	020
Sister Roberts	Shaklon	026

They also had a word code to identify certain situations or people:

Chubuk	Move quickly
Temon	OK, relax
Adom	Male
Kiz	Woman
Sen	You are being watched
Trick	Traitor
Rebs	Police
Chucks	White folks
Eli	Assemble-prepare for immediate action
Jehu	Destroy or attack
Chokee	Freeze

(These and other extensive radio codes were retrieved from a dump by the sheriff's department.)

The patrol group used CB radios to stay in contact. In general, the patrols used standard police codes with a few modifications. On one page of codes recovered from the dump, deputies discovered the 10-13 "help code" which was followed by the words: "Saint needs help."

Once, while monitoring the security patrol's transmissions, deputies used the ten-thirteen code several times throughout the night. Every time they used the code, reinforcements poured from the houses, jumped into cars, and raced to aid in the non-existent emergency.

During this period of increasing tension, both the Cochise County Sheriff's Office and the Arizona Department of Public Safety were keeping a close watch on the church and its activities. For example, the DPS gave the sheriff's department a dossier on most church members and their previous (if any) police records. The intelligence gathered by the state indicated that they and the local Cochise County authorities were beginning to see trouble on the horizon.

Among those who saw the growing problem firsthand was the county attorney's office investigator, John Barnes. In November of 1980, Barnes was in Miracle Valley questioning church members and residents. On his way out onto Highway Ninety-two, he was followed by one of the patrols.

Barnes stopped his car and walked to the security patrol car that had pulled up behind him. Upon asking why he was being followed, he was confronted with force. Four-armed patrol members leaped from the vehicle. They screamed threats at him and racial epithets. One man fired a shot into the air. A coolheaded Barnes put his arms up and walked slowly back to his car. He drove away, and to his relief he wasn't followed.

When deputies investigated the incident, a white resident told them, "We have been, basically, prisoners within our homes." At this point, many whites in Miracle Valley were feeling the heat of a growing militancy from the CMHCC. Charges of racism were constantly hurled at residents—both white and long-time black residents. The church members were intimidating citizens and government officials alike—flaunting the law at every opportunity.

The racial conflicts and issues that were testing the country's resolve and character had come to Cochise County. But there was a difference—the sheriff's department was dealing with a radical religious group—a cult fueled by racism. In a time of riots, racial violence, and political correctness, Sheriff Jimmy Judd and his deputies were walking a tightrope.

There were many deputies of Mexican descent that knew about racism firsthand, such as Deputy Vince Madrid—and he found the charge of racism especially onerous. Clearly, Cochise County had a long history of multi-culturalism.

To meet the challenge, Judd ordered Deputies Ray Thatcher, Bill

Townsend, and Vince Madrid to begin foot patrols along the streets of Miracle Valley and the CMHCC compound. Their purpose was to be certain the church members did not forget that there was indeed law in Cochise County. Judd hoped the officers' presence in their midst would be sufficiently convincing.

Endnotes

[1] Ray Thatcher had been an investigator for the Cochise County Sheriff's Office working out of the Sierra Vista Substation for two years. He was asked if he would like to volunteer for duty in Miracle Valley. Thatcher jumped at the opportunity, hoping he might "help the people."

[2] This warning system later developed into a beacon light and siren. When police cars would enter Miracle Valley, the signal would go off, and people exited their homes to come to their fellow church members aid. Interview with Sergeant Buddy Hale, March 8, 2008.

Chapter Eleven

Screams in the Night

IN APRIL OF 1981, after a month of agony, six-year-old Theriel Drew finally screamed himself to death.

Non-church-member neighbors reported to deputies that they had heard the child's cries on and off for some time. Finally it was too much to ignore. Ray Atchison, a longtime resident of Miracle Valley and neighbor of the Drew family had to do something. "I heard the little boy screaming death cries," reported Atchison. "I tried to talk with the mother, but you could see the fear her own church put in her."[1] Others tried to intervene, but were told to mind their own business.

School Superintendent Brust remembered Theriel Drew, one of the earlier arrivals from Mississippi, as "A fine little man—well behaved and smart."

Dr. R.C. Froede performed the autopsy and determined that Theriel had been suffering from a strangulated hernia for three or four days. He called the death of Theriel Drew "Total neglect."[2] He reported the findings to authorities of the state child welfare system. The Drew boy was the fifth such death of a child at the church compound since their arrival less than two years earlier. At least four of these deaths could have been prevented had medical treatment been sought.

Unanswered Prayers

But no treatment had been sought. The Christ Miracle Healing Center and Church performed their own healing. They had prayed over Theriel Drew. Pastor Thomas prayed. Her son, Bishop William Thomas, Jr., prayed. The boy's parents prayed, and during services in the church, they all prayed. But their faith and prayers weren't enough and the boy died. He died of a horribly painful death due to the strangulated hernia.

The Cult

Perhaps some of the most telling insight into the CMHCC and Pastor Thomas's total control over her followers was to come from a black social worker from the Arizona Department of Economic Security. Robert Conley, Jr. had grown up in the ghettos in Cincinnati and lived around the corner from Muslim groups in the 1930s and 1940s. Conley, Jr. had served twenty years in the military, received a degree in economics, and after being trained had a second career as a social worker.

In an earlier visit to Miracle Valley, Robert Conley, Jr. (and a coworker named Mwandishi) asked Mr. and Mrs. Drew about the health of the surviving Drew children. The parents denied their request for a doctor to examine the children.

On June 15, 1981, Conley made another attempt to get permission to have the Drew children examined by a doctor. He realized that Pastor Thomas controlled the CMHCC and its members and decided to bypass the Drews. Little did he realize to what extent Pastor Thomas dominated her parishioners.

Conley, Jr. and a coworker named Jay McEwan drove to the church in Miracle Valley and found it locked. Conley, Jr. then proceeded to Pastor Thomas's house. It was not hard to find. The domed, blue house was the largest one in Miracle Valley and was rumored to contain an indoor swimming pool and expensive furniture.[3]

The state employees pulled up in front of the pastor's house and were immediately blocked by cars in front and behind them. Conley stated the purpose of their visit and waited in the car for one-half hour. He was becoming nervous. He was then instructed to drive to the church, accompanied by several cars. At the church half a dozen young men, including William Thomas, Jr., escorted him inside.

Conley, Jr. and McEwan were seated at a small table. They were surrounded by the men and felt very intimidated. Conley struck up a conversation with William Thomas, Jr. He explained why they were there and thought he was "developing a rapport" with the bishop.[4]

Pastor Thomas surged into the room from a side door. She was angry and began reciting biblical verses. The "rapport" he thought he had with the bishop evaporated instantly. Conley and McEwan found themselves surrounded by a dozen people and a very determined preacher. He stated the reason for their visit—the Department of Economic Security wanted the surviving Drew children to be examined by a doctor. Conley added that if they were not successful in coming to an agreement, the state would probably petition for a court order.

The response was powerful. Pastor Thomas, among "amens," "yes's" and more "amens," declared in no uncertain terms that they were "not going to take [the church members'] children." She declared, "If you think Jonestown was a picnic, you haven't seen anything yet." [5] Thomas further threatened to kidnap white children if black children were taken out of Miracle Valley.

Conley took Thomas's words with deadly seriousness. He was amazed at her control over her followers. It surpassed anything he had witnessed in the ghetto growing up—far beyond the Muslim groups he had seen during his youth. He left fully believing Pastor Thomas was capable of leading her parishioners in mass suicides, kidnapping, or violence. Robert Conley, Jr. left Miracle Valley never to return. He drove directly to Bisbee and reported his encounter to the Cochise County Sheriff's Department and his superiors. [6]

In late June of 1981, state child welfare authorities served notice on John and Willie Mae Drew, informing them that the authorities intended to supervise the care of their other four children. The Drews were ordered to appear in court—an order they ignored.

More Threats and Courts Intervene

In early July, Sheriff Judd, accompanied by a group of deputies, entered Miracle Valley to confront the Drews. The sheriff anticipated resistance from church members, but not to the extent they received. Upon their arrival at the Drew home, angry men and women immediately surrounded the officers and loudly announced their displeasure. Sheriff Judd and his deputies were told, "We'll die before we give up our children, and if you try to take them, you'll die first."

Judd again served the court order to the Drews and departed with his men without further incident. The case was headed for court.

This time the CMHCC hired an attorney, which began a year-long period of legal wrangling. The case was taken to the Cochise

County Superior Court. The church had one defense—a powerful one in the eye of the court. Divine healing was a foundation of the church members' beliefs, and, as Pastor Thomas testified, if a child died, it was clearly the will of God—a law above all others. The Judge agreed. He ruled against the state in favor of the Drews' beliefs, halting any action by the state child welfare agency.

But it didn't end there. An appeal was immediately filed by child welfare and the State Attorney General's Office with the Arizona Court of Appeals.

In December of 1981, the appellate court reversed the Cochise County Judge's decision. The court ruled the state did have sufficient cause for concern about the possible medical needs of the four remaining Drew children; the court stated reason to declare the children State dependents. This would have resulted in child welfare scrutiny of the surviving Drew children had it not been for another appeal. The church's attorney appealed to the Arizona Supreme Court.

In a ruling by the Arizona Supreme Court, handed down in May of 1982, the appellate court's decision was reversed. The justices ruled that the religious beliefs of the family took precedence over the concerns of the state. The only exception would be in the event of clearly demonstrable danger to the children, in which case the state could intervene.

Unfortunately for the children, such danger could virtually never be discovered—certainly not in time to make a difference in their lives. Child welfare was not monitoring them since it had been officially precluded by the Supreme Court.

Complexities

The case of Theriel Drew's tragic death illustrates the complexities of the issues at work in Miracle Valley. Not only was there the clear case of the church and its members threatening residents and flaunting the law, but there were also constitutional issues. Among these issues were freedom of religion and, as we will see later, the right to bear arms.

Clearly, Mrs. Thomas and the members of the Christ Miracle Healing Center and Church allowed Theriel Drew to die a horrible death. Some, possibly all, truly believed he would be healed by God and if he succumbed (as did four other children), it was God's will. It was just meant to be.

However, in addition to being a megalomaniac, if Pastor Frances Thomas was a knowing charlatan as was her mentor, A. A. Allen, then she was guilty of much more than neglect and the wrongful death of the children.

The various courts of Arizona differed in their opinions, which cuts to the crux of the issue. It comes down to a matter of opinion. There are people who devoutly believe in the power of divine healing—many claiming they have witnessed such events. Others believe equally strongly that these events are nothing more than hocus pocus. But in either case, the five children of Miracle Valley were still dead, and when the legal dust finally settled, the espoused beliefs of the Drew family and the CMHCC were reinforced and given a greater impetus.

Endnotes

[1] The Arizona Republic, October 25, 1987.

[2] Interview with Dr. R. C. Froede, September 18, 2008.

[3] According to an interview on February 22, 2006, with Captain Bert Goodman, Pastor Thomas had two houses. The large domed house according to Goodman contained a lot of very expensive furniture— most of which was covered by sheets.

[4] Deposition of Robert Conley, December 6, 1983.

[5] Deposition of Robert Conley, December 6, 1983.

[6] Deposition of Robert Conley, December 6, 1983.

Chapter Twelve
Diplomacy and Roadblocks

BY JULY OF 1981, the situation in Miracle Valley was reaching a boiling point. Other than Sheriff Judd's visit to the church months earlier, the angry encounter over the Drew children was his first real encounter with church members and finalized all his developing concerns. He'd taken deputies into the valley on the assumption that a small show of force would defuse the church members' typical response. But while no violence occurred, the members' attitude was clear and the sheriff and his men had been told they would die if they tried to take the children.

Governor Bruce Babbitt. Photo courtesy of the Arizona Daily Star.

Governor Babbitt Counsels Restraint

It was that encounter that stimulated the sheriff into his first meeting with Governor Bruce Babbitt and DPS (department of public security—highway patrol) Director Ralph Milstead, with whom he had already had discussions.

Sheriff Judd believed it was time for Arizona's governor and largest law enforcement agency to become fully aware of the situation in Miracle Valley, as well as the conditions the sheriff and his men were encountering on a daily basis. It was also Judd's hope that they would be in a position to offer advice, counsel, and possibly assistance.

The governor advised a calm approach—keep things quiet. But Judd believed more was required. The last thing he wanted was an increase in tensions. However, Judd believed that this group, with their tendency toward confrontation, intimidation, and violence, needed to understand that they were not above the law as they so stated.

During a previous conversation with Milstead, the DPS Director had agreed to Judd's request to assign a black officer to his force. Milstead assigned Thad Hall to the sheriff's department. Hall was to ride along with deputies so that church members would see a black presence in local law enforcement. The church had called the department racist and redneck many times, and the sheriff hoped Hall's presence would be a demonstration of cooperation.

It was Hall who stated, "The blacks [CMHCC members] did not respect authority. Especially when it's coming from whites. I don't know if it would make any difference if it were coming from blacks either. But [in] dealing with the whites ... I can totally say—because of the actions that I saw with the blacks there—they were not going to respect any law enforcement." It was clear that Hall did not think Pastor Thomas had any respect for the law.[1]

Even though Sheriff Judd had been advised to go-slow and "keep a lid on the situation," Pastor Thomas and her group were becoming more confident and militant.[2] By July of 1981, not only was the church's policy of armed patrols well established, but they were initiating a policy of armed roadblocks.

Armed Roadblocks

Robert Ronislz, a civilian employee at Fort Huachuca, stated that in early July 1981, he and his wife were enroute to Bisbee at approximately 10:45 PM. While approaching Miracle Valley on Highway Ninety-two, the couple observed several vehicles blocking the highway. Since Ronislz thought there might have been an accident, he pulled his vehicle off the road, stopped, and asked if he could help.

As he stopped, a car moved in front of his vehicle and stopped. Moments later, another car pulled in behind his vehicle—blocking him in. Ronislz observed several black men, one of whom approached his vehicle and told him to get on down the road. He believed he and his wife were in imminent danger. As soon as the car in front of him moved, Ronislz left the area.

This was not an isolated incident. On other occasions, cars were stopped with roadblocks on the highway. In one case, a woman was traveling through Arizona with her daughter and pulled over on Highway Ninety-two—she was warned she didn't belong and told to get out.

Harassment by Church Members

On July 10, 1981, two separate incidents of harassment by church members were reported.

Eugene Morreau, an APS (Arizona Public Service—electric company) employee stated that on the afternoon of July 10th, he was in Miracle Valley at the Evans' residence, checking the power he had turned off the previous day. The seal had been broken and the power turned back on. He attempted to climb the pole in order to shut off the power source. Approximately fifteen church members surrounded him. He was told that under no circumstance would he be allowed to disconnect the power. Morreau replied that Evans had been properly notified of the impending disconnection. One person in the crowd ended the discussion with, "You must not want to live very long doing the kind of job you're doing."

Paying the Bills

Many church members worked at some type of job at least intermittently. It was well-known that Pastor Thomas collected most of her flock's income so she could "care" for them. She assured her people that the church had indeed paid the electric bills on their behalf and that the APS man's attempt to shut off the Evans' power was simply one more racist act by the white establishment from which she was working so hard to protect them. APS records showed that power bill payments were sporadic at best and often not paid at all.

In addition, the CMHCC would buy clothes at thrift stores and use food stamps to buy food for their members. The church's erratic payment of their members' bills led to frequent conflicts.

Sergeant Don Barnett and Deputy Rod Rothrock responded to a call to rescue an APS man. When they arrived, they found him on the power pole surrounded by fifteen angry, shouting, threatening church members. The officers heard one man shouting, "We'll shoot you off that pole." Another shouted, "We'll shoot." Under the protection of the deputies, Mr. Morreau left with all possible haste. He had not been allowed to do his job. The power at the Evans' residence remained connected.[3]

Karen Huber, a Miracle Valley resident, reported the second incident of the day. At about 11:00 PM, as she was taking a youth-group member to her home in Miracle Valley from a church function, two vehicles attempted to force her to stop near the CMHCC. She was frightened, and turned off Highway Ninety-two into the campus of the Arizona Bible College. She sought refuge in one of the buildings and observed a security patrol car repeatedly drive through the campus area.[4]

After that incident, Huber was afraid to enter the valley at night and no longer held any church functions for which she had to furnish transportation.

Babbitt Reconsiders

Things were obviously becoming more difficult and even though the governor was reluctant, Judd's request for action prevailed. On July 17, 1981, Director Milstead deployed DPS officers and vehicles to Miracle Valley. The DPS and sheriff's department amplified their patrols of the area. It was their intention to make it clear that they would no longer tolerate the violent and completely unlawful behavior that had become standard operating procedure for the cult.

But that's not what happened. Church members became even more militant—confronting officers at every opportunity. Altercations became regular and shots were occasionally fired.

White residents were blockading themselves in their homes—concerned for their physical welfare, due to the increasing clashes between church members and law enforcement officers. It was a situation that was unacceptable to Sheriff Judd. It was his jurisdiction and he was determined to restore peace to Miracle Valley, by whatever means required. Meanwhile, from a distance, deputies used binoculars to maintain a constant vigil on the church and the area.

Judd again approached Governor Babbitt and brought up the subject of calling in additional reinforcements; Judd even broached the subject of using National Guard troops. There were hundreds of well-armed church members who had proven their willingness to employ armed force in response to any provocation. Judd's number of deputies, even bolstered by the DPS, had made no impression on the church.

A Memorandum of Understanding

The governor denied his request and again advised Sheriff Judd to take a calm, quiet approach to the church. Judd, who preferred peace to confrontation, made the decision to accept the governor's recommendation. On July 20th, 1981, the sheriff convinced Pastor Thomas to sit down and talk with him in Sierra Vista.

At the meeting, on more than one occasion, there were loud voices across the table. However, after two days of negotiations, Sheriff Judd and Pastor Frances Thomas came to a number of agreements.

Pastor Thomas and her son William Thomas, Jr. agreed to get along with their neighbors. She consented to have her flock keep any weapons locked away. She agreed to develop a better relationship with the deputies in Judd's department and to avoid confrontations. She also said she would end roadblocks on the highway. Finally—and of critical importance—the pastor declared that she would cancel all security patrols throughout the valley—armed or otherwise.

The sheriff agreed to use dialogue instead of force. He pledged that his people would take the church's concerns seriously and actively investigate any complaints or problems. Further, he agreed that his deputies would be instructed to take a more subdued approach to any minor problems with church members. He also consented to hire a black deputy or at least establish a greater black presence within his department.

The News Conference

Sheriff Jimmy Judd and Pastor Frances Thomas had come to whatever agreements that were possible. Although the sheriff had more than enough justification for his skepticism, on July 23, 1981, he sat at a table with Pastor Thomas. They faced residents, newspaper reporters, and a line-up of television cameras. The time had come to bring positive news and a message of hope to the community. They announced the results of their successful negotiations and their written declaration of peace which they termed a "Memorandum of Understanding," which detailed the agreements. Then each made a declarative statement affirming the positive approach that they both intended for the future.

Sheriff Judd stated, "What's happened in the past should be forgotten. A new day has dawned today, and I think we should go on from here."

Mrs. Thomas offered, "What has happened has happened, but we're looking forward to a brighter day and to a better communication between the people in Miracle Valley."

At the end of the news conference, the memorandum was signed in full view of everyone present. Sheriff Judd and Undersheriff Dale Lehman signed for Cochise County. Mrs. Thomas and her son signed for the Christ Miracle Healing Center and Church.

The Result

The peace they affirmed that day never truly existed. The sheriff's skepticism had been well founded. Judd did instruct his people to maintain a hands-off approach to minor offenses, and Milstead agreed to keep black DPS officers on the sheriff's staff. Judd met his end of the bargain. But to Mrs. Thomas and her people, the negotiation had been only so much air. The peace didn't last a week.

In Sheriff Judd's view, the key feature was already being violated. Non-church residents of Miracle Valley reported seeing security patrols.

On the first of August, two school signs inflamed the church members, who were true to their militancy. On the signs, two illustrated children wore sweaters—one with the letter "N," and the other with the letter "A." The church members interpreted the letters to mean "Nigger" and "Asshole." There was never any explanation from the Department of Transportation, but the sheriff saw to it that the signs came down immediately.

But the removal of the signs wasn't enough. The church members took the offensive and increased their complaints of racism at the elementary school. They claimed their children were in constant, mortal danger from the other students and racist teachers. In protest, they temporarily pulled all of the church's children out of the Palominas School.

Endnotes

[1] Sacks, Status Report CIV 82-343 TUC_ACM.

[2] Interview with Bert Goodman, February 23, 2006.

[3] July 10, 1981—Facts from Incident Report:

Sgt. Barnett received a call to rescue an APS (Arizona Public Service-Electric Company) man (Morreau), having problems with HC (Healing Center) members. Upon arriving Barnett found a white man surrounded by fifteen blacks. The man had turned off an HC member's electricity for non-payment and the blacks were threatening him to turn it back on. He had earlier turned the power off and someone had turned it back on. No one touched the APS man, but he felt threatened. When Barnett told the group they would be arrested if they tried to stop an APS man from doing his job, they laughed at him.

[4] Taken from: Office of the Attorney General, Inner-Office Memo, Subject: Prior Bad Acts. Written June 27, 1983.

Chapter Thirteen

The Guns of August

Substation

During the second week of August, 1981, in order to manage the increasing tension in Miracle Valley, the sheriff's department opened a substation. It was a small house about two football fields from Pastor Thomas's large blue house.

From the substation, they could monitor any activity on a continual basis. The station was manned by two deputies, twenty-fours a day, and managed by Deputy Ruben Leon. These were nervous times for the deputies. While they monitored the cult, the cult monitored them. The substation was under constant surveillance by church members—who saw to it that the deputies knew they were being watched.

Dusk to dawn was a spooky time in the small house. Car horns and voices throughout the night reminded the deputies they were being observed and the constant fear was that armed churchmen might attack. The potential was not imagined. The church members' behavior had proven that. A week after the substation was established, sympathetic border patrol agents loaned the sheriff a number of electronic perimeter sensors, which were placed strategically around the substation. If trouble came, the men inside would now have at least some warning.

A Well-Armed Church

As noted earlier, church members were arming themselves. Defenders of Pastor Thomas have declared that this was not against the law—after all, this was Arizona, and the Constitution guaranteed the right to bear arms. Nonetheless, the Arizona Department of Public Safety was monitoring the arms buildup and checking to see if any of the church members with felony records were buying weapons. The mixture of guns and a militant cult concerned the State of Arizona and Cochise County Sheriff Jimmy Judd.

The DPS turned over to Judd an extensive list of weapons purchased by church members—below is a partial list of the weapons.

Church Member	Weapon
William Thomas, Jr.	Stainless Steel Model 19 357 Cal. Revolver
Gus Gillespie	.32 Cal. Revolver
Amos Thompson	.38 Cal. Revolver
Ray Charles Carter	.45 Cal.Semi Thompson
Kenneth Tyrone Evans	.20 Ga. H&R Shotgun
Keith Thurman	.20 Ga H&R Shotgun
Julius Gillespie	.30 .30 Winchester Model 94
Billy Dean Bernard	.30 .30 Winchester Model 94
Keith Thurman	.38 Cal. R&G Spec. Revolver
Keith Thurman	.20 Ga. Shotgun
Marv Lois Thompson	.32 Cal. S&W Revolver
Roy E. Williams	.38 Cal. R&G Revolver
Percy L. Pipkins	.22 Cal H&R Rifle
Percy L. Pipkins	.30 .30 Winchester Model 94
Sherman McCane	.25 Cal. Titan Auto
Nancy Tate	.38 Cal. R&G Special revolver
Percy L. Pipkins	.22 Cal. H&R Revolver
Amos Thompson	Case Amogel Dynamite + 50 Blasting caps
Wade Dean Morrison	.22 Cal. Rifle
Ray Charles Carter	.38 Cal. R&G
Willie Carson	.25 Cal. Raven Auto
Don Jones	.25 Cal. Raven Auto
Reboyce Smith	Chemicals
George Smith	Case Amogel Dynamite + 100 Delay Blasting caps
Robert Lee Brooks	.38 Cal. R&G 2" Revolver
James W. Pipkins	.38 Cat. R&G Revolver

Church Member	Weapon
Steven Lindsey	.30 Cal. Carbine
James Triplett, Jr.	.30 Cal. Carbine
Frank Bernard	.30 Cal. Carbine
Frank Bernard	.38 Cal. 6 Revolver
Sherman McCane	.30 Cal Carbine
William Thomas, Jr.	.30 Cal Carbine + 6 30 round clips
Keith Thurman	.30 Cal Carbine
Robert Lee Luckett	22. Cal. R&G Revolver
Ray Charles Carter	.38 Cal. Rohn
Cornelius Hanger	.20 Ga. Shotgun

Financial Concerns

In a radio interview given by Pastor Thomas, she indicated that the church received funding from tithes and offerings.[1] It appears that there were also other sources of income available to the church. In a deposition given by teenage church member Willie Triplett, he mentioned working as a janitor at the elementary school and turning most his wages over to Frances Thomas. She would then give him an allowance of twenty or thirty dollars to compensate him for his two weeks of work at the school. He stated that he didn't like it, but everybody did it.[2]

In addition, the state was investigating food stamp and welfare fraud by church members. It was alleged that church members would receive welfare checks at a state office (for example, in Bisbee) and then go to another office (in Benson or Sierra Vista) and get another check. This was allegedly exposed when a state worker from Bisbee filled in at an office in Benson. A woman from the church that this employee had known by one name appeared in the other office under a different name.

It has also been reported that at one point as many as one hundred church members were collecting unemployment. At that time payments averaged slightly over $180 every two weeks. This would have amounted close to $36,000 a month, which was also turned over to Pastor Thomas.[3]

Finally, Cochise County Deputy Ray Thatcher reported that William Thomas, Jr. was often out of Miracle Valley. He said that Bishop Thomas would drive church members to Sierra Vista and Tucson in his 1979 black Lincoln to peddle flowers on street corners. The money was turned over to the church. While this doesn't seem like a very lucrative practice, Gus Gillespie once noted that when church members sold flowers in Chicago the revenues averaged approximately two to three hundred dollars per person. [4]

Despite these income sources, the CMHCC was apparently encountering financial problems, as illustrated by the inability of the church to pay the electric bills of some of its flock. This is most likely a result of the legal expenses of the court cases resulting from the Drew tragedy and other lawsuits that were to follow. Another expense was the church's purchase of property from residents that were leaving Miracle Valley because of (among other things) harassment. It is interesting to note that the CMHCC never applied for tax exempt status in Arizona. [5] Apparently, all revenue went to Pastor Thomas and not the church. Despite their financial issues the church continued its arms build up.

An Armed Camp

In late July of 1981, Cochise County Sheriff Deputies noticed increased activity around the church's swimming pool. The pool and its facilities were surrounded by a high concrete block wall. Typically, there were few people at the pool since there were issues with the pump.

Suddenly, the pool was a beehive of activity. The pool was guarded twenty-four hours a day by members of the cult's armed patrol. The gate leading into the facility was locked. All of this was unfolding when Sheriff Judd was negotiating the "Memorandum of Understanding" with Pastor Thomas.

In August of 1981, there was even more activity. Rumors began to fly. The DPS and ATF were convinced that there was dynamite being stored at the pool. It wasn't illegal, but it was an escalation in the threat level that the CMHCC presented.

Hank Murray, out of the Tucson ATF Office, decided to take the direct approach. In order to appear non-threatening, he drove into Miracle Valley alone and parked in front of the church owned gas station. He went into the station and told the attendant he was from the ATF and wanted to inspect the dynamite. Pastor Thomas was called and in a matter of minutes was at the store. An unhappy Thomas asked, "What do you want white boy? [6]

Murray explained that he needed to check to see if they were complying with Federal regulations regarding the storage of dynamite. Thomas consented and Murray was led to a storage room at the pool. Inside was the dynamite. Murray informed them that the door to the shed had poor hinges and the lock was inadequate. He told them he'd be back in a week and if the door was not fixed, he would confiscate the dynamite. When he returned in a week the door met Federal standards. Unfortunately, he couldn't confiscate the dynamite.[7]

As he left Miracle Valley, he wondered what the church intended to do with the dynamite. It would not be long before everyone found out.

Endnotes

[1] According to a 1981 radio interview of Pastor Thomas.

[2] Willie Triplett Deposition October 11, 1984.

[3] Interview with Buddy Hale, March 7, 2008.

[4] The Arizona Republic, October 25, 1987.

[5] Interview with Bill Breen, August 27, 2008.

[6] Interview with Hank Murray, September17, 2008.

[7] Interview with Hank Murray, September17, 2008.

Chapter Fourteen

Palominas School Revisited

The Parking Lot Incident

On August 24, 1981, a meeting of the school board was in progress at the Palominas School. Since the school had become a focal point for the church's hostility, sheriff's deputies monitored it throughout the day. On this day, it was Sergeant Don Barnett who spotted George Smith—a church member who was known to all the deputies from previous clashes—drive into the gravel parking lot outside the school. Smith sat alone in his car watching the building.

After a few minutes, Sergeant Barnett approached the car and asked Smith what he was up to. When the man didn't reply, Barnett asked again. Instead of responding with words, Smith gave Barnett a nasty look and gunned his engine.

Sergeant Barnett jumped back a step to keep from being hit as the car roared out of the lot. In the process, the car pelted Barnett painfully with flying gravel from both spinning rear tires. Smith clearly knew what he was doing. He could have backed off the accelerator, but didn't. He watched Barnett being pelted in the rear view mirror as he spun out of the lot.

It was a deliberate attack on a deputy by a church member and Sergeant Barnett had more than enough just cause for an arrest. He ran to his patrol car and took chase, lights flashing and sirens blaring.

The Christ Miracle Healing Center and Church compound was only two miles away and Smith headed straight for it. By the time he pulled in and stopped in front of the church building, Sergeant Barnett's car was right behind him. Smith stayed seated in his car. Barnett got out of his vehicle and approached Smith.

A small crowd was gathering.

Barnett ordered George Smith out of his vehicle. Smith refused, saying, "I ain't going nowhere." Again Barnett ordered him to exit the vehicle. Again Smith refused.

Barnett threw open Smith's door and began pulling him out. Smith held onto the wheel and planted his feet. He had no intention of letting the deputy wrestle him from the car. Smith was yelling now and so was the growing crowd.

Without warning, Barnett was hit from behind. He spun around to find that he was surrounded by about thirty yelling church members. He was being grabbed from all sides. A large screaming woman began pummeling him in the face. He tried unsuccessfully to block her blows—there were hands all over him. He spotted a flash of light reflected off a metal object and tried to back up as another woman began slashing at him with long scissors. From behind, Barnett was being jabbed and regularly hit with rocks, and all the while screaming voices reminded him how close he was to death. "You're gonna die white boy," people screamed. "You gonna die today." Spit was flying and the mob was growing.

Clearly, getting out of there before the crowd made good on their threats—which was beginning to look like a very real possibility—was the only reasonable option for the deputy. There was one of him and an army of them. They were already doing damage. He was cut and bruised and it could only get worse.

Barnett managed to wrestle himself free from the mob and bolted for his car. They pelted him with rocks as he ran, and they continued to throw things at the car as he drove away.

August 25, 1981

Sheriff Judd knew he could not allow this obvious attack on one of his men to go unchallenged. George Smith had to be arrested. Judd also knew the cult was heavily armed and, counting the women who had shown themselves to be an eager part of their force, they numbered at least two hundred and fifty.

The sheriff first called DPS Director Ralph Milstead. He asked for DPS support. Milstead turned him down. He said he didn't want his officers taking orders from Judd or any of his people, clearly implying a lack of confidence in the sheriff. But there was more to it than just that: Milstead had his own agenda.

Milstead was brusque when he spoke to Judd. He was brusque when he spoke with any of Arizona's fifteen county sheriffs. Milstead ran the statewide highway patrol and it is reported that he had never made any secret of his desire for his organization to become a full-fledged state police force—subordinating all the sheriffs and police departments in the state. Here was an easy opportunity, simply gained by not providing support, to allow a county sheriff to possibly get himself in over his head.

Sheriff Judd calls Milstead. Photo courtesy of the Arizona Daily Star.

If Judd made a mistake, Milstead's own position would be strengthened. He could point a finger and call the sheriff incompetent. This would be one more example of why Arizona needed Milstead's organization to become bona fide state police. Before Milstead ended the conversation with Judd, he passed the buck, telling Judd he couldn't provide help without the approval of Governor Babbitt. Judd told him he'd be calling Babbitt. According to Judd, Milstead said, "Be my guest."

Sheriff Judd's next call was to Governor Babbitt. He explained the situation and stated, as he had many times before, "No one is above the law." But it seemed, where the cult was concerned, the governor wanted them to be above the law. He again urged the sheriff to maintain a hands-off policy. The sheriff told the governor that would be impossible in this case. He restated the large number of people he might face and asked for DPS assistance. Governor Babbitt refused.

It was becoming apparent Milstead might not have been the only one with a personal agenda. Something was up with the governor. The rumors had been flying for some time that Governor Babbitt was grooming himself for a presidential bid. He had power, influence, and financial backing. What he lacked was minority support, and it was said that he had met with Jesse Jackson, looking for help.

While Judd wasn't about to make any accusations, it certainly seemed possible that Babbitt's insistence of a hands-off policy (in spite of the group's continuing violence and flaunting of the law) was, at least, very suspicious. Perhaps the governor was running his decisions through a presidential-election-committee before committing to them.

With or without the support of the governor or DPS, Cochise County was Sheriff Jimmy Judd's jurisdiction and decisions about how to deal with lawless elements on his turf were still his to make. George Smith was going to be arrested.

The sheriff called in promises of support from the Sierra Vista and Douglas Police Departments—departments that had had their own violent encounters with the church on many occasions. With their help, Judd mounted a force of fifty officers and over thirty vehicles.

Officers and vehicles took up positions around and inside Miracle Valley, on the road and the highway. Many deputies were on foot. Sergeant Larry Dever's SWAT team was positioned in the fields surrounding the compound. There was no attempt at concealment. It was the show of force the sheriff hoped would keep the cult at bay. With his people in place, the sheriff announced they were there to arrest George Smith. And then they waited.

It was the sheriff's intention to make a "show" and not engage the church members. If they were forced to eventually search for and then take Smith by force, Judd was prepared to do so, but only as a last resort. So, they waited.

Judd's force held its position for one day, then two. During this time, church members milled about quietly and stared at officers. They seemed intimidated, which was the sheriff's intention, and made no aggressive moves.

At the end of the second day, a door in the church building opened and George Smith walked to one of the nearby patrol cars and quietly surrendered. People watched from porches and roadways, but there was no yelling and no church member made any of their customary threats.

When the car carrying Smith had cleared the valley and was on its way to the jail in Bisbee, Sheriff Judd ordered his men to stand down. For once, an encounter with the church had ended uneventfully. Judd had been right—with sufficient numbers, a show of force was clearly a successful tactic.

The following day, Smith appeared before a judge and was allowed to pay a fine and return to the church.

Chapter Fifteen

The Militant Mother and Son

THE CHURCH MEMBERS MAY have been quiet when they gave up George Smith, but calm never lasted long, and public and private statements were taking on an even more militant tone.

Harold Hurtt, a black Phoenix police captain, was frequently used by Milstead and Babbitt in their dialogues with the Christ Miracle Healing Center and Church. He was often called "the governor's mediator." Hurtt met with Pastor Thomas shortly after the George Smith incident. He stated publicly, "Some of the conversation changed to more of a militant attitude. You know, [they said] 'if we're going to stay, if we have to fight, if we have to die, we will do that.'"

Growing Militancy

Mrs. Thomas told the press, "Those people call us niggers and we're supposed to run. But these niggers are not going to run. They try to make us look like criminals. We will stand our ground."

The increasing militancy was obvious in the writing and actions of her son, William Thomas, Jr., a Bishop in the church and their "military leader" who practiced martial arts and with firearms daily. On one occasion, Bishop Thomas and his "Commandos for Christ" were practicing on a gun

William Thomas Jr. often declared he was willing to die as a martyr. Photo courtesy of the Arizona Daily Star.

range near Miracle Valley. Pastor Thomas was an observer—after a while the she told the shooters to remember to "aim at the heart and the head."[1]

William fancied himself a poet and wrote: "Death sings a sweeter song and plays a softer tune than the cold, iron chains of slavery."

In an excerpt from his poem entitled *Fight or Flight,* he wrote: "We are a humble people, bringing the things we could carry, our last pennies we have spent, buying homes, even trailers, anything we could afford just to have a place for shelter. Peace and harmony we offered. They came into our church and we made them welcome there. Then, from beneath their smiling faces, came the anger hidden deep. They watched our homes, harassed our children, and followed behind us in the street. Should we stay and give a fight or give up what's our own? Should we stand up and be recognized or bend beneath the white man's bar?"

William, Jr. distrusted and hated his white neighbors. He did not hate them as badly, however, as he hated the representatives of law enforcement; his disdain for the sheriff became increasingly obvious in his writing.

"So, I find Hitler [referring to Sheriff Judd] is very much alive and well in Cochise County and I say it is to you Hitler, who disguises himself as our county official. It is you who judges us today, but it is God who judges you tomorrow."

"We have been branded as a cult because they say we are chanting. We are said to be lunatics. I find they have conspired to re-oppress and enslave us as they have the Indians and Mexicans."

Much of his poetry echoed a recurring theme. He often prophesied his death at the hands of law enforcement and declared that he was prepared to die. For all of his hate and paranoia, he must have believed in a god and heaven. William Thomas, Jr. made it very clear that he looked forward to dying a martyr. He often said that he believed he'd be killed by Cochise County law enforcement. He publicly stated this in an August, 1981, meeting: "If that is the way I have to go, I'm ready to be martyred. It is their plan to harass us, intimidate us, and kill us if necessary and to drive us from the face of Cochise County."

Trash Cover—Part One

Trash covers are one of the most unappealing methods that information can be gained regarding people and organizations. The retrieval of documents, pictures, and evidence from discarded material, AKA garbage, can supply a treasure trove of information. In general, the CMHCC members were very careful with their trash. When they did let their guard down Deputy Rod Rothrock was there.

The "Saints Place" was a two story structure located on Highway 92 two or three buildings east of the church. It was used as a day care center. Rothrock noticed church members dumping their trash in cans near the building. As he was on patrol late at night he would periodically stop and look through the garbage.

As noted earlier, the codes that the church's security patrol used were recovered by Rothrock. More importantly, he discovered material that was discarded from the day care activities.

Among these items were eight virtually identical pieces of paper, all drawn by the hands of young children. Since they were found together, they were likely created at the same time. The words were bold and laid out in the shape of a cross—with the vertical and horizontal bars sharing a common letter—and read: "WHITE MEN YOU WILL WISH YOU WERE NEVER BORN."[2]

When School Superintendent Brust speculated earlier that these youngsters were attending a school at the church that instructed them in the art of hate and paranoia, he was more correct than even he had suspected. The education of hate began at an early age.

Trash Cover—Part Two

Another trash cover effort was proceeding on a much larger scale. Bill Breen was a former deputy with the Cochise County Sheriffs office. He had been hired by the same man that brought Jimmy Judd on board as Undersheriff years before—Sheriff Jim Willson. Before the trouble began in Miracle Valley, Breen joined the Southern Arizona Narcotics Strike Force. Shortly after that, Bill Breen became an investigator and analyst for ACISA (Arizona State Criminal Intelligence Systems Agency).

ACISA Investigator Bill Breen (center) began his career as a Cochise County Sheriff's Deputy. He is shown with Captain Bert Goodman (left) and Deputy Doug Knipp (right).

When the routine traffic stops in Miracle Valley started escalating into major confrontations Judd brought Breen into the picture. From that point on Breen supplied intelligence to the Cochise County Sheriffs Department and County Attorney Beverly Jenny. As part of his effort, Breen turned his attention to the CMHCC garbage. Pastor Thomas and William Thomas, Jr. were careful, to the point of paranoia. Pastor Thomas had a large flat bed trailer parked in an empty lot in Miracle Valley. The sides of the flatbed were built up with sheets of plywood attached to metal poles. The church members would dump almost all their trash and garbage into the walled flatbed trailer. After four or five weeks of cooking in the Arizona sun, the stinking trailer was hauled to a landfill.

Unknown to Pastor Thomas, Breen was always notified when the truck left Miracle Valley. Breen would rush to the landfill and have the dozer operator open a new trench for the "Miracle Valley" trash delivery. The trash from the church was always dumped in a "pristine" trench so it would not be contaminated by other debris. Then the dirty work started.

Pulling on thick rubber gloves, Bill Breen and four or five officers from DPS would sort through the trash. They would dig through diapers, fermenting food, broken glass, nails, oil cans, batteries, rags and clothing. As the day grew hotter they continued searching for information. Maggots swarmed over them—crawling up the legs of their pants. Every one of the law officers would periodically take time out to vomit. Breen and his crew persisted. And the persistence paid off.

Among the documents recovered were essays, poems and plays written by students in the church school. The theme throughout the writings was that "white people are devils" that only want to enslave them or kill them. The students wrote how they would turn the tables, kill the whites and take their property—rejoicing over the bodies.

Two documents caused an immediate call to Sheriff Judd from Breen.[3] The first document was an extensive list of "targets" in Cochise County. It included a map showing where the targets were located.

They were part of a contingency plan that the church would institute under certain circumstances. A partial list of targets included: [4]

» Cochise County Courthouse and Jail
» Cochise County Juvenile Detention Center
» Bisbee Police Department
» Sierra Vista Police Department
» Telephone switching stations
» Electric power stations
» Gasoline storage tanks
» Bridges on Hwy. 80 and 92 to cut off access to southern Cochise Co.

Sheriff Jimmy Judd stands in front of the Cochise County Courthouse and Jail. It was on a list of "targets" to be blown up.

The second document included the tactical plan for taking out the targets. This included the number of people required, weapons needed and the amount of dynamite to use to blow up the targets. Breen turned these documents over to Sheriff Judd and Lieutenant Dale Lehman within twenty-four hours.

Other material Bill Breen and his crew uncovered was heartbreaking. As noted earlier, Pastor Thomas received most of the money earned by her church members and provided them with the amount that she felt they needed. It fell short of their needs. Many discarded letters were from church members pleading that Pastor Thomas increase their stipend.

One letter begged Pastor Thomas for "forty dollars so I can buy food for my family" and get "my stove fixed."

Finally, Breen recovered many documents concerning the beliefs of the cult. Among them was the Commando for Christ Pledge.

Commando for Christ Pledge[5]

I am a Commando for Christ. I serve in the force of Holiness which guard the Saint's and God's valley and our way of life. I am prepared to give my life in their defense.

I will never surrender of my own free will to any enemy or devil. If in command, I will never surrender my brethren while they still have the means to resist.

If I am captured I will continue to resist by all means available. I will make every effort to escape and aid others to escape. I will accept neither parole nor special favors from the enemy.

If I become prisoner of this war, I will keep the faith with my fellow prisoners. I will give no information nor take part in any action which might be harmful to my comrades. If I am senior, I will take command. If not, I will obey the lawful orders of those appointed over me and will back them up in every way.

When questioned, should I become a prisoner of war, I am not bound to give any information. I will evade answering further questions to the utmost of my ability. I will make no oral or written statements disloyal to my god and my allies or harmful to their cause.

I will never forget that I am a Commando for Christ, responsible for my actions, and dedicated to the principles which made the valley. I will trust in my God and His place of refuge, Miracle Valley.

A Subtle Change

As the militancy of the church grew, so did the prominence of William Thomas, Jr. Bishop Thomas was the leader of the armed security patrols and was exerting increased influence everywhere within the CMHCC organization. Proof of his rise was to be seen in the church itself. Behind the altar, the large picture of Pastor Thomas had been replaced by that of Bishop William Thomas, Jr. [6]

Endnotes

[1] Triplett Deposition October 11, 1984.

[2] Interview with Rod Rothrock, September 1, 2008

[3] Interview with Bill Breen, August 27, 2008.

[4] Interview with Bill Breen, August 27, 2008.

[5] "Commando for Christ Pledge," by William Thomas, Jr.

[6] Interview with Edna Judd, August 23, 2008.

Chapter Sixteen

The Chartier Incident

September 7, 1981

Deputies Al Tomlinson and Rod Rothrock were patrolling along Highway Ninety-two on the afternoon of September 7, 1981, when they spotted dust trails up ahead. The clouds of dust could only come from a number of vehicles moving along the unpaved streets of Miracle Valley.[1]

As the deputies pulled up to the scene, six church security vehicles were parked blocking a pickup truck. The church members were already out of the cars and dozens of others were rushing from the compound area toward the vehicles. The deputies parked and moved toward the group. Heavily armed church members (men and women)—some with pipes, rebar and, clubs, and many with rifles and pistols—were screaming at the pickup. Fifty or more church members quickly surrounded the deputies and the truck. While the purpose of their anger was unclear, screaming men were, according to Deputy Rothrock, "Up in [their] faces. [The screaming men] were so angry, Tomlinson and [Rothrock] had a lot of reason to be concerned for the two people in the truck—a man and a woman—and, frankly, for [their] own safety." Then it got worse.

One of the occupants of the pickup, a Bisbee woman named Phyllis Chartier, leapt screaming from the truck. She was as angry as the church members and yelled in retaliation. "Ain't no niggers gonna tell me where I can go."

The pitch of the church member's anger rose exponentially. Several lunged at Chartier, swinging clubs. So far she wasn't hit. Rothrock and Tomlinson moved in to protect her. Neither deputy had any respect for the endangered and apparently intoxicated woman's conduct. In fact, they had as little respect for her as they did for the threatening behavior of the church members. But she was the one in imminent danger and they had a job to do.

Rothrock did what he could to hold the church members at bay. Tomlinson moved to protect Chartier who was still screaming racist epithets at the church members. "Why don't you niggers go back to where you came from! You give them a little bit of authority and they try to take over."

Churchmen lunged, but didn't connect with Chartier. "For a while," said Rothrock, "We thought, seriously, this might be it. We thought we might die that day."

Tomlinson managed to force the still-yelling Phyllis Chartier back into the truck while Rothrock held the angry blacks at bay. Chartier was minimally protected in the truck.

Tomlinson turned to help Rothrock—trying to effect calm or anything close to it. It was then that a churchman identified as Sherman McCane stepped forward, still enraged by the incident. He approached Deputy Tomlinson, screaming close to his face. This was the kind of behavior designed to provoke violence. The deputies had witnessed this many times before.

Tomlinson stepped back. He told the man to back up and calm down, which angered McCane even more. A still-screaming Sherman McCane threw a punch at the deputy, catching him squarely in the arm. Tomlinson took another step back. McCane moved in and hit him with a second roundhouse punch to the upper arm. McCane moved into the crowd. Tomlinson began speaking to the group, calling for calm, and asking them to explain what had happened.

The situation was still serious, but what Rothrock calls, "Tomlinson's spontaneous negotiation" was beginning to have an effect. The inflamed church members continued yelling, threatening to kill the "piece of shit, white woman." But weapons were being lowered.

Comments were made about the pickup having no business driving through their valley. The church members claimed that they responded because they'd heard shots being fired, knew the truck's occupants were armed, and moved to protect themselves. At this point, what they said was considerably less important than the fact that they were speaking instead of shooting or swinging clubs. There was still more than enough anger to go around, but the level of potential violence was dropping.

A second sheriff's vehicle arrived, carrying Deputy Doug Knipp and Thad Hall, a black DPS Officer (as we have noted) who had been loaned to the sheriff's department specifically to add a black presence.

Rothrock and Tomlinson hoped Hall's appearance might calm things. They were wrong. Hall was a member of law enforcement and certainly not a member of the church. Being black had no positive effect. Rothrock and Tomlinson were on the inside of the angry mob. Knipp and Hall were outside the heavily armed group that had no intention of allowing anyone to get any closer. The law enforcement men tried to edge their way nearer.

The deputies kept Chartier and her husband contained in the pickup truck while they continued to speak to the group. Eventually, they convinced a church member to move one of the vehicles, which allowed the pickup to escape the area—escorted by Knipp and Hall.

Rothrock credits Tomlinson with diffusing that situation: "People could have easily died that day, including us. Al did an incredible job." [2] They had indeed rescued the Chartiers, but the struggle wasn't over.

The group had not dispersed, but the mood had changed from a mob mentality—fifty people all screaming at once—to a lower level of' complaining, punctuated by angry outbursts. A sullen Sherman McCane watched.

The deputies were faced with a dangerous decision. One situation had been defused, but they still faced the problem regarding what to do about McCane's assault on Tomlinson. McCane was ready to do further battle. The deputies had full cause for an arrest, but the crowd was prepared to become a mob again, and the deputies were severely outnumbered and very badly outgunned.

These were experienced law enforcement officers who had been in difficult and dangerous situations before. There was only one logical decision. They continued to ask for calm and reason, announcing, "This must end now. We don't want anybody hurt here today."

Even the church members recognized the volatility of the situation. Much of the poison had drained from many of their veins, and McCane was one of only a few who were still exhibiting such anger. Several of the churchmen spoke quietly to McCane. After a few minutes, with only a long glance backward at the deputies, he disappeared deeper into the crowd. The mob did not disperse but slowly began backing off.

It was the opportunity Rothrock and Tomlinson needed to make a strategic retreat. They entered their car and slowly drove out of the area. No arrests were made that day, and more importantly, no one was severely injured or killed. Circumstances were only an instant away from the flash point that could have become a blood bath, were it not for the restraint and courage of two Cochise County deputies.

Endnotes

[1] Taken from: Office of the Attorney General. Inter-Office Memo, Subject: Prior Bad Acts. Written, June 27, 1983.

Facts: Deputies Tomlinson and Rothrock saw a car block the road out of Miracle Valley and another car drive up to the roadblock and stop. George Smith (Christ Miracle Healing Center and Church member) got out of the first car and a white male got out of the second. The deputies approached the two. More CMHCC vehicles drove up.

A white woman from the second car called the blacks "niggers." A shoving match ensued among the civilians and the deputies intervened. The deputies escorted the whites back to the second car.

Sherman McCane approached Deputy Tomlinson. Tomlinson told him the deputies would handle the situation and asked McCane to remain calm. McCane hit Tomlinson's arm twice. The whites were allowed to drive away. The blacks dispersed.

[2] Interview with Rod Rothrock, September 22, 2006.

Chapter Seventeen

The War Wagon

September 10, 1981

The Chartier incident culminated with the attack by Sherman McCane on Deputy Al Tomlinson. It was not something that could be allowed to slide. It had been a highly volatile situation, and the deputy had been physically assaulted. Cochise County Attorney Beverly Jenny, a "country lawyer" who didn't put up with nonsense, filed charges against McCane in Cochise County Superior Court. An arrest warrant for assaulting an officer was issued.

Sherman McCane would be arrested. Despite numerous previous offenses, arrests of church members had been infrequent. This was often because the perpetrator had been difficult to identify. The church members, who assumed the whites were unfamiliar with blacks and would have difficulty identifying them, enhanced that concept by dressing alike. The men, many of whom were tall and thin, usually wore long-sleeve black shirts and denim pants. The women, many of whom were relatively short and stout, often wore red blouses and blue skirts. It was a well thought-out attempt to confuse identification, which had obviously worked.

In addition, state authorities (including Milstead and Governor Babbitt) had repeatedly cautioned authorities in the county to show restraint—a policy that was evident from the earlier "Memorandum of Understanding" signed by Sheriff Judd and Pastor Thomas. However, Sheriff Judd realized this last incident had crossed the line.

Shoot the Radio

Since the chance of serving a warrant inside Miracle Valley held the strong opportunity for another violent flare-up, Sheriff Judd made the decision to have McCane picked up the following day at his place of employment—an exterminating company in Sierra Vista.

The sheriff's department was represented in Sierra Vista by a small substation, manned by three or four people, including the second-in-command of the county's SWAT unit, Sergeant Buddy Hale.

Sergeant Hale was sent to arrest Sherman McCane. When Hale and his partner started to take McCane into custody, the man tried to open his briefcase. Inside the case were a knife and a .25 automatic.[1]

They transported McCane to the Sierra Vista sheriff's substation. He was booked on the assault charge and for carrying a concealed weapon. Word quickly made its way to Miracle Valley. Within an hour of McCane's arrest, William Thomas, Jr. and churchwoman Dorothy Collins[2] arrived at the substation demanding to see McCane.

That did not happen. Instead, Sergeant Buddy Hale heard an ominous rattling inside a large purple handbag carried by Collins. With just cause to assume she might be hiding a weapon, he confiscated her bag. Inside were numbchucks—possession of which is illegal in Arizona. Collins was immediately arrested.[3]

William Thomas snarled, "Are you going to arrest me?"

Sergeant Hale replied, "Are you carrying a concealed weapon?"

The situation was turning tense. Hale took his deputies aside and instructed them that "if a mob of people come through the front door, shoot the radio and retreat out the back." The attackers would not be able to intercept communications, and the lawmen would make a stand in a more defensible position.

At this point, Sherman McCane demanded his single phone call. Around five PM, a church van that had become known as "The War Wagon" pulled out of Miracle Valley, followed by another vehicle.

As noted earlier, there were five or six people in the van when it left the valley on its ill-fated mission. Two were in the middle seat, including Brother Gillespie and a young woman. Frank Bernard was behind the wheel, and Steven Lindsey, age twenty-five, was in the front passenger seat. In the rear seat was another man and perhaps another woman. They were well armed and on their way to Sierra Vista. In addition, another vehicle containing three or four church

An Earlier Encounter with the War Wagon

School Superintendent Gene Brust received his first death threat shortly after his last encounter with the five churchmen in his office (see Chapter Seven). A voice on his phone declared, "We're killing you today, Brust."

Brust, who lived in Bisbee at the time, noticed that the gray War Wagon, with three or four men in it, was following him to and from school every day. Brust informed Sheriff Judd what was going on. In the mean time a couple of Brust's friends came to his aide. Will Sparks, a big, no-nonsense man, stationed himself along the route Brust took to school. In addition, a hunting buddy started following the War Wagon to school. Shortly thereafter, Brust was making the trip to school without being trailed.

The respite was short lived. Palominas Principal Byron McGough borrowed Brust's black Blazer to go to Sierra Vista. On his return he declared to Brust, "Never again will I take your Blazer. Those people followed me all the way into Sierra Vista, sat there while I got supplies, and then followed me all the way back to Palominas School."

Soon after Brust received another phone call saying, "I'm going to kill you." Brust wasn't too concerned because the "issue hadn't exploded yet," but in the back of his mind he thought "it just might."

Brust was returning from Sierra Vista a few days later and looked in his rearview mirror as he was going through Ash Canyon. He saw the War Wagon coming up behind him—fast. He looked for something to defend himself, but he didn't have a gun. Brust counted four men in the vehicle and noticed the front passenger window being opened. He thinks, "For crying out loud, I'm in trouble."

The van starts to pull around Brust, who considers slamming on his brakes to throw off the aim of the shot he's expecting. The War Wagon pulls up along side of Brust. A man leans out the window and points a finger at him—he mouths the words, "Bang, bang," as the War Wagon passes. The Superintendent called Sheriff Judd and said, "Jimmy, if I had a gun I'd been shooting. I thought I was going to get shot."[5]

From then on Superintendent Brust took the threats much more seriously, and the Sheriff initiated increased patrols around his home.

members followed closely. Their intention was to remove McCane from custody by violent means—and for that they were very well prepared.[4]

Boom!

Several miles outside of Miracle Valley tragedy struck. There was an explosion. Smoke poured from the War Wagon as it continued for half a mile and ended up off the road in a field. The trailing car pulled up and stopped. The occupants of the car ran to the distorted remains of the war wagon. Passing motorists reported seeing weapons being removed from the van and people being helped into the car.

On that day, Deputy Rod Rothrock was partnered with Deputy Doug Knipp, which was an interesting coincidence as they were two of the four officers involved in the Chartier incident that resulted in the arrest of Sherman McCane. They were on routine patrol when they received a call to investigate a traffic situation—possibly an roll over—along an open stretch of Highway Ninety-two between Miracle Valley and Sierra Vista.

When they arrived on the scene, they were greeted with a curious set of circumstances. There was what the deputies referred to as "a debris field" in the roadway. They found twisted metal parts and fluids from a vehicle. There were no other people in the area. A short distance away, the van they knew to be The War Wagon sat in a field. They could tell from experience that the van had rolled (not rolled over) rather than driven to that location. They also knew the van had come from the church, and past incidents had taught them to proceed with caution.

The first thing that was readily apparent was that something catastrophic had happened to the vehicle. It was misshapen. The roof was shoved up and the windows blown out. There was also a peculiar odor lingering in the air. Before they reached the van, Deputy Knipp, who had worked for one of the local mines years before, speculated it was an odor he recognized. It smelled like dynamite.

They approached the van cautiously from the back, looked in the rear windows, then walked around to the passenger side. What

The War Wagon rolled off the highway into a field.
DPS photo used in investigation.

Most of the windows were blown out and the roof was shoved upward.
DPS photo used in investigation.

was left of Steve Lindsey was hanging out. A leg jammed between the front passenger door and seat with the rest of his body heaved back—suspended out the open double door on the passenger side. Lindsey had been eviscerated and his hands were essentially missing.

Bomb squad

Backup arrived quickly upon the grizzly scene, led by Captain Bert Goodman. The captain immediately notified Sheriff Judd, who, in turn, called Sergeant Paul Larimer. Larimer headed the DPS Cooperative Enforcement Unit (CEU).

Bart Goodwin from the DPS Crime Investigation Bureau had been in Sierra Vista when he heard of the explosion. He raced to the scene. Since the "crime scene" stretched along State Highway Ninety–two, he quickly started the process of getting approval to shut down the highway. He also arranged for medical examiner Dr. R. C. Froede and Will Seddon (chief mortician—investigator) to helicopter to the scene. Dr. W. Birkby, a forensic anthropologist and Dr. J. Beyers, a co-medical examiner would arrive that evening by car. Dr. Froede, Dr. Birkby and Dr. Beyers were also on the faculty of the University of Arizona in Tucson. [6]

Larimer's team soon arrived on the scene. His unit investigated liquor and narcotics cases and was available to other agencies upon request. Before the wrecker hauled the van off to a secure lot for further examination and the ambulance took Lindsey's mangled body to the morgue, Larimore and his unit took control of the investigation. One of the finest investigators in the state, Herman Flores started to scour the scene.

The Sheriff's office helped shut down the road and detour traffic, while Larimer's crew gathered evidence. Among the evidence along the highway were body parts and mangled weapons. [7] While they found no evidence of shotguns, it was obvious there had been rifles and hand guns in the van. They also found evidence that somebody had removed much of the firearm evidence before the van was discovered by Deputy Rothrock and Deputy Knipp.

DPS bomb expert Ed Stock arrived. There might still be bombs in the vehicle. He declared it was too dangerous to proceed until morning. In the dim glow of the Arizona sunset a helicopter sat down near the crime scene. The forensic experts, like everyone else, would have to wait until tomorrow to process the van. The highway would be closed all night.

(Left to right) Bart Goodwin, Bill Seddon, Dr. R. C. Froede and Herman Flores examine debris field. DPS photo used in investigation.

First Light

At first light, the investigation into the explosion began in earnest. As the processing of the scene continued, Sergeant Larimer began to receive calls from Phoenix. Ralph Milstead, the head of DPS wanted to talk to him. Larimer ignored the calls. He and his men continued their investigation. The media observed the proceedings from nearby.

Dr. Birkby and Bart Goodwin watched as Dr. Froede leaned into the van from the driver's side and Herman Flores did the same from the passenger side. At the same time Flores and Dr. Froede sighted another dynamite bomb. A split second later from inside the van, bomb expert Ed Stock yelled, "We have a live one!"[8]

The area around the van cleared almost instantly. Dr. Froede recalled Herman Flores clearing a four or five foot fence without effort.[9] Flores noted that the nationally renowned Dr. Froede led the way. Ed Stock stayed put and defused the live bomb. If the bomb had gone off everyone near the van, including the media would have been killed or injured. Stock found another bomb under a seat and completely intact. A third bomb, damaged by the explosion was also discovered.[10]

Undamaged bomb recovered from the War Wagon. DPS photo used in investigation.

The calls from DPS Director Milstead's office continued—and they continued to go unanswered by Larimer. He had a job to do and he would not be interrupted.

Damaged bomb removed from the War Wagon. DPS photo used in investigation.

By mid morning, ATF personnel arrived from California. Larimer blocked them from entering the crime scene. No one was going to contaminate the scene or hinder his unit's investigation. Only when his men said it was okay did he allow the ATF access.[11]

At two-thirty on Friday afternoon, the highway was reopened. It had been shut down twenty-four hours.

Command Performance

Larimer decided it was time to take a call from the DPS. Ralph Milstead wanted to see Larimer and Herman Flores in

View of interior from driver's side. DPS photo used in investigation.

Bart Goodwin inspects passenger side of van. DPS photo used in investigation.

Dr. Froede (left) watches Ed Stock (center, in van) gather evidence. DPS photo used in investigation.

the morning—first thing. Larimer and Flores drove to Phoenix early
the next morning.

Sergeant Larimer and investigator Herman Flores sat across
the table from Director Milstead, Deputy Director Sam Lewis and
several other DPS officials. Flores presented preliminary information
on what they had discovered. It would take time for a full-fledged
report. Milstead and Lewis started pushing. They wanted answers
and they wanted them now.

The questions about the investigation quickly moved to "when can
we expect an arrest?" Milstead, looking directly at Flores, demanded
"I'd like to have an arrest by next week." The straight talking Larimer
had had enough. He responded to Milstead, "Just because a van blew
up near Miracle Valley, doesn't mean the Constitution went out the
window." He continued, "It takes time to develop evidence and to
arrest someone so charges will stick."[12]

Faulty Detonator

The investigators made several determinations. Steven Lindsey
had been cradling a bomb in his lap when it exploded. It was constructed of four half-sticks of Amogel Dynamite taped together in a
block. It was rigged with a tripwire detonator, which was constructed
of a clothes pin with two thumb tacks facing each other on the inside
tips. Wires were soldered to the tacks and the wires lead to a battery
to provide the spark for detonation.

The tacks were held apart by a metal clip to prevent the clothes
pin from closing and making contact. The clip could easily be
attached to a string or piece of fishing line so it could be removed
from a distance or set-off by being stumbled over. In that case, it
would be know as a "tripwire detonator," which is customarily used
in booby traps.

It also could be called a "suicide detonator," so named because
the separator can also be removed with the fingers and is favored by
bombers interested in blowing themselves up in the process.

Even if Lindsey was suicidal—for which there was no evidence—
he was on a mission to the jail to break out Sherman McCane, and
there were four of five others in the van with him. The bomb experts
speculated that Lindsey was in the process of arming the explosive

device when it blew. Sergeant Larimer noted, "He (Lindsey) was good at chemicals, but poor with electricity."[13]

The body of Steve Lindsey is removed from the scene of the explosion.
Photo courtesy of the Arizona Daily Star.

Though the investigators had found three more bombs that were identical to the one that had killed Steve Lindsey, there had been more bombs. If Deputies Rothrock and Knipp had arrived on the scene a few minutes earlier, they would have found much more.

Pastor Thomas Reacts

Less than an hour before the van blew up, Frank Bernard had asked eighteen-year-old Willie Triplett if he wanted to ride along in The War Wagon to get Sherman McCane and Dorothy Collins out of the Sierra Vista Sheriff's substation. He declined, and it saved his life.[14]

Thirty minutes later, the injured occupant's of the van were re-entering Miracle Valley. Young Triplett was on his way to a church service when he heard the news. Outside the building, Gus Gillespie was talking with Pastor Thomas—The War Wagon never reached Sierra Vista. Gillespie said, "The van blew up. Steve [Lindsey] was killed." A very upset Pastor Thomas replied, "Quit lying. He's not dead."

Church member Ray Charles Carter jumped in his vehicle and

sped toward the accident scene. A few minutes later, he drove back into Miracle Valley and picked up Triplett. The pair went to the large swimming pool owned by the church, and Triplett helped him unload two boxes of bombs into the pool storage shed. They took another box of bombs "to Steve's sister's house." [15]

Denials and Details

Pastor Thomas began to make denials. She declared there were no weapons in the van. However, witnesses saw weapons being removed from the van and Dr. R. C. Froede saw a handgun in the debris field.

The DPS continued their investigation. Bart Goodwin interviewed the van occupants that survived the explosion. It was not easy. He met Pastor Thomas who agreed to let him have access to the survivors, but under controlled conditions. He interviewed them in Pastor Thomas' church. They were heavily supervised.

The woman who sat directly behind Steve Lindsey when the bomb went off, was still emotionally distraught when interviewed. She said, "The worst part of the explosion was having to swallow two mouthfuls of Brother Stevie."[16] It is reported she vomited frequently for days after the incident.

Despite the difficulties, the DPS was putting the pieces of the story together. The DPS investigation confirmed the occupants of the War Wagon and the following car were on a mission to break Sherman McCane and Dorothy Collins out of the Sierra Vista substation. The plan was to create a distraction in the substation, while bombs were planted under patrol cars. The bombs would then be detonated. When the deputies left to investigate the explosions, the perpetrators would blow a hole in the side of the substation, freeing McCane and Collins.

DPS and ATF explosive experts quickly established that the dynamite was part of a purchase of a case of Amogel Dynamite and one hundred blasting caps made by churchmen Amos Thompson and George Smith on July 12, 1981, from the Apache Powder Company in Benson, Arizona.[17] At that time, it was fairly easy to purchase dynamite in Arizona. A person had to have identification and a legitimate reason to purchase it—the most common reason being that they were working a claim on their property. [18]

Dynamite and Detonators

As noted earlier, it had been determined earlier that the church stored dynamite at their swimming pool facility in Miracle Valley. After the van explosion DPS Sergeant Paul Larimer entered Miracle Valley and drove to the pool. The usually well guarded complex was quiet. The gate to the concrete block wall that surrounded the pool, dressing rooms and storage shed was wide open. Larimer entered the storage shed and determined there was still some dynamite unaccounted for.[19] He confiscated the remaining dynamite from the shed.[20]

In an equally unusual event, Bart Goodwin and some other investigators went to a chili pepper canning plant on September 16, 1981. It was known that church members worked at the Douglas, Arizona plant. In looking through the plant's trash, the unit recovered over a dozen bomb timers and clocks.[21] A backpack was among the items found. The pack appeared to have fresh blood on it. It contained six alarm clocks, clothespins and wire. It was believed to have been associated with the dynamite bomb that exploded on September 10. It was also believed the backpack had been in the van at the time of the explosion. [22]

Bart Goodwin searches for evidence. DPS photo used in investigation.

Investigators uncover a backpack full of clocks. DPS photo used in investigation.

Shortly after the incident, Pastor Frances Thomas addressed the matter during a radio interview. When asked to explain the circumstances surrounding the dynamite explosion that destroyed the War Wagon, she replied, "I can't explain anything about it, because we didn't have any [dynamite] on there. There was nothing on [the War Wagon] ... mostly but kids, except for Brother Julius and Brother Frank. They're young adults and these men know nothing about the dynamite at all. If there was some on there, we know nothing about it and we did not have any on there." [23]

Pastor Thomas was asked, "Does the church own a mine in Cochise County?" She declared, "I don't think foolish questions should be asked." When pressed that she had earlier said that dynamite was used for mining purposes, she shifted gears. "What I said was the truth," she responded. It is interesting that Steven Lindsey was never mentioned as having been in the War Wagon.

A Home Visit

In order to identify the fingerprints found in the War Wagon after the explosion, federal subpoenas were issued for nine or ten of Pastor Thomas' flock. The subpoenas were for certain individuals to appear in Tucson to be fingerprinted. It fell to ATF Agent Hank Murray to serve the subpoenas. Murray headed for Miracle Valley with DPS investigator Herman Flores.

Murray drove to Pastor Thomas' large blue house and parked in the yard. A very irritated Frances Thomas emerged with four or five heavily armed guards. The first words out of her mouth were, "White boy, you'd better get of my property while you still can."

Murray responded, "I'm here to serve some subpoenas."

"You aren't serving no papers on nobody, white boy," she answered. "I think you should leave while you can."

Murray told Thomas that he'd be back to serve the subpoenas after he talked to the U.S. Attorney in Tucson. Murray and Flores left and went to the Sierra Vista DPS headquarters to phone Tucson. As Murray was on the phone with the U.S. Attorney's Office, Frances Thomas called. She told Murray he could come back and serve the subpoenas. Thomas asked, "Who do you want to see, white boy?"

When he returned to Miracle Valley the people he wanted to serve with papers were waiting at the gas station for him.[24]

Despite Pastor Thomas's denials, Frank Bernard, who had driven the War Wagon the day of the explosion, later plead guilty to federal bombing charges. Since his fingerprints were found on the internal components of the bombs, any defense he could have mounted would have been weak.[25] He was sentenced to six months on a work farm. When he completed his sentence, he returned to Miracle Valley.

Endnotes

[1] Interview with Buddy Hale, March 7, 2008.

[2] Dorothy Collins is not to be confused with Dorothy Williams who was a member of the CMHCC's Security Patrol and the commander of one the force's "flights."

[3] Taken from: Office of the Attorney General, Inner-Office Memo, Subject: Prior Bad Acts. Written June 27, 1983.

> Facts:

> Dorothy Collins and William Thomas, Jr. and another woman came to the Sierra Vista Substation to ask about Sherman McCane, who had been arrested earlier. Ms. Collins had a bag that rattled from the sound of wood sticks hitting.

[4] In an interview on August 12, 2008, Virgil Judd revealed that one of the survivors of the explosion said, that in addition to freeing McCane they wanted to kill Sheriff Judd. They had been told the Sheriff was at the substation.

[5] Interview with Gene Brust, May 5, 2006.

[6] Interview with Bart Goodwin, September 9, 2008.

[7] Interview with Paul Larimer, September 4, 2008.

[8] Interview with Bart Goodwin, September 9, 2008.

[9] Interview with Dr. Freode, September 9, 2008.

[10] Interview with Bart Goodwin, September 9, 2008

[11] Interview with Paul Larimer, September 4, 2008.

[12] Interview with Paul Larimer, September 4, 2008.

[13] Interview with Paul Larimer, September 4, 2008.

[14] Triplett Deposition, October 11, 1984.

[15] Triplett Deposition, October 11, 1984.

[16] Interview with Bart Goodwin, September 9, 2008.

[17] ATF Form 4710—Transactions Dated July 12, 1981 and August 6, 1981.

[18] Sacks, Status Report CIV 82-343 TUC_ACM.

[19] Interview with Bill Breen, August 27, 2008.

[20] Interview with Paul Larimer, September 4, 2008.

[21] Interview with Bill Breen, September 9, 2008.

[22] Sacks, Status Report CIV 82-343 TUC_ACM

[23] According to a 1981 radio interview of Pastor Thomas.

[24] Interview with Hank Murray, September 17, 2008.

[25] Sacks, Status Report CIV 82-343 TUC_ACM.

Chapter Eighteen
The Aftermath

The Funeral

After the autopsy, Lindsey's body was released to a local funeral home, placed in a coffin, and taken to the Christ Miracle Healing Center and Church for a proper ceremony. No outsiders were allowed at the service for one of their "saints." According to the church members, Steven Lindsey had perished on a noble errand for God. The story Pastor Thomas told her congregation had little to do with a fallen saint. It had everything to do with his rebirth by her divine countenance.

She preached that she had resurrected Steve Lindsey, and that the closed coffin at the front of the altar was in fact empty. The funeral was a celebration of the resurrection of a man she called "a virgin soldier of God." This was another excellent example of the level of control she commanded.

Thomas certainly couldn't produce Steve Lindsey alive. So one of her stories was that after bringing him back to life—whole and healthy—she had sent him away to Los Angeles for his own safety. Since the white man's law would certainly arrest him on sight, Thomas further instructed the flock not to seek him out.

That same law would likely follow any church member in an attempt to find Lindsey, which is precisely why Thomas, as part of his resurrection, had also altered his appearance. In that way, Lindsey could not be found by anyone, even fellow church members, and would stay anonymous until Thomas deemed it safe for him to return to Miracle Valley.[1]

September 15, 1981

The explosion had far greater effect than just an increased concern on the part of law enforcement. Widespread anxiety rippled through the community. Residents were now seriously concerned. Many had seen churchmen carrying handguns and rifles. Many had seen them practicing with their weapons. Some nearby residents had shots fired near their homes by the armed security patrols. The patrols had now clearly demonstrated their possession of explosives and their willingness to use them.

For days after the bombing event, the sheriff's department received nonstop calls from residents of the area. Based on recent events, their concerns were well justified. Many were terrified. Parents were, in fact, so frightened about their children's welfare—and knew how often problems had occurred at school—that many residents kept their children at home.

At an emergency meeting—recognizing the serious potential danger—the Palominas School Board made the decision to temporarily close the school.

The Sheriff Makes His Case

Once again, Sheriff Judd called upon Governor Babbitt and Ralph Milstead (head of the Department of Public Safety), and this time Judd refused to listen to suggestions of maintaining a calm, quiet attitude. A churchman had died a violent death, by his own misdeed, on the way to break two of Pastor Thomas's flock out of jail. The school had closed and residents were both terrified and angry. Action had to be taken. Judd's case was undeniable, even by a reluctant state administration.

Sheriff Judd insisted on DPS assistance, and this time he received it. Milstead deployed officers and vehicles to the area. They set up roadblocks on Highway Ninety-two on both sides of Miracle Valley, which effectively sealed it off. No one entered or left the valley without being stopped. Cars were inspected, and, at least temporarily, the cult was contained.

The pressure in the community against the CMHCC was growing. Miracle Valley Estates residents Jim Melton, Coy Meeks, Ann Nance, and others were banding together and complaining against "the unequal enforcement of justice and the law."

Four days after the van explosion on September 15th, Sheriff Judd staged a community meeting at the Palominas School. He had taken serious action, but also recognized the need to keep the concerned citizens from taking any action of their own.

Judd emphasized his statements to the crowd: "Other than the incident Friday night, [the van explosion], there have been no deaths.[2] There have been no injuries. There's been no property damage. And as you know, we have taken appropriate action." The sheriff was trying to preserve the peace and protect the public—he was walking a tightrope. The result was that no one was happy—including the average citizens, Pastor Thomas and her flock, Governor Babbitt, and Ralph Milstead.

The frustration of the audience was boiling over. The townspeople expressed their frustration. An unidentified man of about sixty said, "Mr. Judd can't do a cotton-picking thing till somebody pulls a trigger or sets a bomb off. Now he's got to sit in that chair just like everybody else. He can't do a thing, but by golly, I can." The room erupted in a brief burst of applause. "I've been through two wars and I didn't get a scratch. So, it's as good a time as any for me to go get shot, but I'll tell you one thing—they're not going to run over me. And they're not going to come out and stop my car, because I'll have blood all over. And I don't think the community should sit around. I think we ought to give them an ultimatum: shape up or ship out."

In reply to a suggestion of putting one policeman on each bus, one of the mothers spoke her opinion: "What good would one policeman on each bus do, honestly? Every incident has been one policeman or two against a group. Do you really think it's going to accomplish anything except to put more pressure on our children? I want my children back in school and I want them back in school soon. But not until I know they'll be safe."

The roadblocks stayed up for a week, during which time the church members remained quiet. The violent death of Steve Lindsey had drawn too much attention. And word soon leaked to the sheriff that Mrs. Thomas had informed her people that they must keep to themselves and halt any activity that would bring additional attention from law enforcement. Again, the show of force had been effective.

The roadblocks came down, and the school reopened. But the sheriff wasn't about to become complacent. There was too much violent history, and promises of calm and cooperation by the church had never been kept. So, Judd ordered constant surveillance of the church and the school by his deputies. He also informed DPS that he would expect their immediate redeployment if it were again requested.

Fines and Dismissals

On September 21, Sherman McCane (whose attack on Deputy Tomlinson during the Chartier incident had precipitated The War Wagon explosion and the subsequent series of events) appeared before a judge. He was found guilty. His sentence was a $360 fine and time served. Phyllis Chartier was arraigned on charges of disorderly conduct. She cited reasonable justification, and the charges were dismissed.

Endnotes

[1] Interview with Bill Townsend, April 26, 2006.

[2] This point was repeated by Sheriff Judd during 1981 radio interview.

Chapter Nineteen
The Triplett Intervention

January, 1982

The Triplett family had lived in Louisville, Mississippi. They had seven children. Susie Mae McCane, the eldest and now married to Sherman McCane, was twenty-four. Lora was seventeen, then came Janet, age fourteen, Rusa Mae, age twelve, and Robert, age eleven. In addition to the minor children, there was another older sister as well as Willie Triplett. Willie was eighteen (he had been invited to ride along on the ill-fated War Wagon trip to Sierra Vista, but had declined). Their mother had died in a traffic accident in 1977.

At the time Susie Mae decided to spirit her siblings out of Mississippi, they were living with their father, Lester Triplett. Susie McCane was smitten by the cult and believed with all her heart that Frances Thomas was, in fact, God. It was with that deep belief that she smuggled her sisters and brother out of Mississippi and brought them to Miracle Valley.

Their father, Lester, back in Chocktaw County, Mississippi, was a decent man, but he was poorly educated and rumored to drink. He was not happy that his children had been spirited away—a feeling held by a dozen other parents, according to Lester. He began to work his way through the Mississippi legal system to regain his children.

The youngsters had been easy marks. They were impoverished and disenfranchised, and their sister, whom they trusted more than anyone, was offering them the opportunity to go to a beautiful new place and live with God. To the gullible children, that sounded a lot better than being poor and alone in Mississippi.

Susie Mae, claiming her father had never returned home after her mother's death and that she had legal guardianship, enrolled Janet, Rusa Mae, and Robert in the Palominas School. The school documents recorded the father's address as unknown. Lora, seventeen, was enrolled in Buena High School in Sierra Vista along with about twenty-five other church-member teens. The year was 1980.

Lester Triplett's efforts to regain his children through legal channels in Mississippi were going nowhere. He was becoming increasingly concerned for their welfare. He made a number of attempts to make contact, and in every case was rebuffed by the church. He was never allowed to speak with or have any other contact with his children.

"I called this old woman [Pastor Thomas] and she'd say 'you ain't getting no kids, and don't call back to my kids anymore,'" noted Triplett.[1] His misgivings were growing.

He had initially been happy in Mississippi when his children started attending Pastor Thomas's church. His first misgiving with the church occurred shortly thereafter.

Triplett reflected, "They'd say, 'Come on Trip, get saved.' I used to go to church, but it was nothing like theirs. They say they've found Christ. But they ain't found nobody. They may have found the devil. I don't believe Christ would do what they do."[2] Triplett made his decision. He contacted the Cochise County authorities.

Cochise County Enters the Picture

After Triplett had made contact with Cochise County authorities, County Attorney Beverly Jenny met with Gene Brust and the Palominas School Board. It was determined that Susie Mae McCane had misrepresented her guardianship and fraudulently enrolled her sisters and brother. The children were subsequently suspended from school. In addition, another dozen students were suspended because of similar custody issues.

Susie Mae McCane filed suit against the school to re-enroll her siblings, but the court ruled she had committed perjury in trying to establish her guardianship by stating her father's whereabouts were unknown. Therefore, the children were not readmitted.

Shortly thereafter, a new home-school law was passed in Cochise County. The Christ Miracle Healing Center and Church qualified under the new law. The Tripletts, along with the rest of the CMHCC's elementary school age children, attended school at the church.

By the end of 1981, Lester Triplett was still in Mississippi, but he

Sinister Allegations

Not only did Lester Triplett feel that his children had been taken away from him illegally, he felt they were being alienated from him—brainwashed. However, there are indications that the children that belonged to the tight-knit Christ Miracle Healing Church and Center may have been suffering more than mental abuse.

Triplett's son Robert is reported to have said he and his siblings would go two or three days without eating and then "all we would get is bread and water."[3]

In addition to hunger and sleep deprivation (because of marathon church services), it was a well-known fact that "monitors" would "whack" children with long sticks when they dozed off in church. Robert also is reported to have said, "They would take the children, tie them up, and whup them for punishment."

A far darker abuse may have been occurring, however. Willie Triplett (his custody was not requested by Lester Triplett because of his age) testified that when he and other children where at Pastor Thomas's house, she asked if she could "check him." Willie reported that Pastor Thomas wanted to check them because she thought they were "fooling around with girls in the church."

According to Willie Triplett, she asked if he "would pull his pants down" so she could check him. Willie declined to be checked. Willie left the pastor's house and didn't know if the other children were "checked."[4]

Whether or not this was a motivating factor in Thomas's strong resistance to having children removed from Miracle Valley is a matter of conjecture.

was then in contact with John Barnes, investigator for the Cochise County Attorney. Triplett wanted his children out of that environment.

Sheriff Judd and Cochise County Attorney Beverly Jenny conferred. Jenny agreed the children were being held by a "guardian" who had no legal authority to do so. In early January, a court order was issued for the children's return to their father—their rightful, legal guardian.

The Sheriff also saw Lester Triplett as an opportunity for discovery. Even with all the contact between the sheriff's department and the church, there was very little solid information about the specifics of the church's operation. Judd authorized the importation of Triplett to Cochise County. He was brought in secretly and put up in a hotel in Bisbee.

The Plan

On the night of January 10, 1982, Sheriff Judd met with Lester Triplett, County Attorney Jenny, Lieutenant Frank Peterson, Sergeant Larry Dever (in charge of the Special Response Team), and several others. A plan was formulated to remove the three younger children from the church and Lora (the seventeen-year-old) from the high school in Sierra Vista.

Lieutenant Peterson would carry two custody court orders for the removal of the three children. One order was to be served at the church school, and the other was to be served on Pastor Thomas, who was expected to be at her residence. Lester Triplett and Deputy Bill Townsend would accompany Lieutenant Peterson in a separate vehicle. Lora Triplett would be picked up at the high school after the younger children were secured.

On the morning of the eleventh, both vehicles entered the valley. Peterson went directly to Mrs. Thomas's house. Townsend and Triplett parked near the store at the corner of Highway Ninety-two and Healing Way, only a short distance from the church. Several churchmen—yelling that the deputy and his companion didn't belong there—immediately approached them.

The deputy ignored their taunts and moved directly to the church. He and Triplett immediately entered the building. There were five semi-circles of seven or eight children and a female teacher at each. The teachers carried four-foot-long switches. One was seen swatting a dozing child. A teacher who was obviously in charge stood at a riser, in front of a group of thirty-five to forty children. She went silent as the two men entered.

Deputy Townsend approached the woman, with the court order in his hand, and explained that he was there to collect the Triplett children. Before she could respond, eight to ten angry black men, including the few from the front of the store, rushed in. The men were yelling and immediately surrounded the deputy and the children's father. Again, as was customary, they were in the lawmen's faces—what Townsend called "nose to nose," and spit was flying.

"Get out!"

"You have no business here. This is our building."

"You have no right. Your bullshit laws don't mean anything here."

"What the hell are you doing here?"

Townsend simply replied, "We are not leaving without the kids."

As the churchmen stayed tight around Townsend and Triplett, yelling in their faces, the women rushed the children from the room to another location in the building. There were no weapons seen, but the yelling continued. Townsend continually interrupted, referring to the court order and naming the children. The churchmen, now bolstered by a few women, yelled back.

"Court orders mean nothing here. This is God's place."

"You are not getting them."

"You are not taking our children."

They yelled at Triplett, "You're just a stinking 'Hank.'"

After close to fifteen minutes, the angry church members had begun to burn out and back off, but not far. Since the children had all been removed, there was no one for Triplett to identify. His children were not there.

At that point, having served the court order on Mrs. Thomas at her residence, Lieutenant Peterson opened the church door and motioned to Deputy Townsend and Lester Triplett—telling them to step outside. As they left the building, they were followed by the churchmen and women, and were confronted by even more people.

There were now at least an additional ten black men and fifteen women, who had not had the opportunity to harass Triplett and the lawmen. The angry rhetoric began anew. The message was the same. Triplett was called a fool and told he was too stupid and "white" to know the church members were saving his children.

After another ten to fifteen minutes outside, Pastor Frances Thomas arrived. She exited her black Lincoln and walked toward the group, which quieted at her approach. The lawmen gave her a moment. She didn't speak. Deputy Townsend announced, "We're leaving with the kids, or thirty deputies will come and get them. I can't believe you want that to happen."

She glared.

Lieutenant Peterson said in a calm but serious tone, "Mrs. Thomas, you've got five minutes—then we're going in."

Townsend was seriously concerned about Peterson's ultimatum. Two men against that angry mob would be somewhere between impossible and suicidal, but a bluff could work; and after a few more moments of stony silence, it did. Mrs. Thomas said to one of the school women, "Bring out the kids."

The group was obviously unhappy with her decision and began to protest, but she was in absolute control of her people and soon had them calmed—announcing, "I'm allowing this. We'll get them back."

The group murmured and milled about uneasily. After a few minutes, the door opened and the woman appeared with the three Triplett children in tow. They were obviously frightened and upset. They were confused and the sight of their father did nothing to appease them.

Their spiritual leader whom they believed to be God spoke to them. "Go with Lester, children," she said. "Go with him now. You'll be back with us very soon."

The children were placed in the rear of Deputy Townsend's vehicle with their father. Townsend drove slowly out of the valley, followed by Lieutenant Frank Peterson, who kept one eye in the rearview mirror.

It had been tense, but the men had the three young ones and managed to extricate them without a violent encounter. It was unknown to the church members that the entire exchange had been observed. Sheriff Jimmy Judd and County Attorney Beverly Jenny were watching the church from the Bible college. Judd was ready to call for backup and send in a SWAT team if the officers needed help.[5]

It should be noted, it is not certain how many backups were present for this operation. SWAT Commander Larry Dever told Deputy Townsend if he was "taken hostage, to stay away from the northwest wall of the church. (The deputies)...will come through the northwest wall." He was referring to the use of a detonating cord.

It looks like rope, but is explosive. It can be stuck to a surface—and then detonated.[6]

As Deputy Townsend turned onto Highway Ninety-two and sped away from the CMHCC complex, he saw several county sheriff vehicles follow him. The deputies transported the kids to the Sierra Vista Sheriff's substation at Foothills Blvd. and Highway Ninety-two—a safe and secure location.

Sergeant Larry Dever deployed members of his SWAT team to the substation; the team was well armed and equally vigilant. Many violent confrontations and the episode with The War Wagon had taught the lawmen to be prepared. It was not known if the church members would try to *free* the children or not. What they might be capable of was anyone's guess.

That left Lora still at Buena High School, where the twenty-five church teens went everywhere in lock-step and had often shown themselves to be every bit as militant as their elders.

The Plan—Part Two

It was a reasonable assumption that Lora Triplett would not smile at her father and come quietly when confronted. She was as indoctrinated as any member of the cult was, and was just as capable of resisting an intervention. She would also be in the company of other church teens, boys as well as girls—since no church member had ever been seen alone under any circumstances. Earlier reconnaissance at the school had shown that to be the case.

Careful preparations had been made by the sheriff (with support from the Sierra Vista Police Department), in an effort to make her extraction as easy and nonviolent as possible. The authorities fully understood that anything could happen, and to assume the experience would be quiet and flawless would have been foolhardy.

With classes underway, students were in classrooms and would be unaware of what may be happening in the hallways. Two deputies took positions near the pay phones to prevent Lora or any of the other church teens from discovering that the younger Tripletts had already been taken. Lora had no knowledge of what had taken place at the church, which Sheriff Judd considered essential to the extraction. Several other deputies and officers from the Sierra Vista Police

Department were stationed in an empty room adjacent to the one in which Lora and other church teens were in class.

Sergeant Dever and several SWAT team members were staged in the parking lot, ready to assist if things got out of hand. They were prepared to go in if required, but acted more as the outside rescue team if the intervention didn't go according to plan.

With all personnel in place, Deputy Bill Townsend, Lester Triplett, and one other deputy left the Sierra Vista Substation in Townsend's car and headed for the school. When they arrived, they joined the other deputies and SVPD officers in the empty classroom, waiting for the bell to ring and class changes to begin. It had been deemed unwise for a group of law enforcement officers to try to operate inside a classroom. Just the time required to properly identify Lora would put the church teens on immediate alert.

The plan was to wait for the students to enter the hallway, at which time Lora's father would make the identification before anyone could become aware of their presence; and then the authorities would quickly take her from the hall.

The bell rang. Doors opened and teenagers began spilling into the hallway. Townsend and Triplett entered the hall, followed closely by the other officers. Lora, in a group of other church teens, was no more than twenty feet away. Her father spotted her almost instantly and pointed her out. Triplett, Deputy Townsend, and one other officer hurried toward her. She saw them coming and realized, just as quickly, they were coming for her, and she bolted.

The other church teens immediately moved to block the officer's paths. They collided. The teens had no intention of allowing Lora, who was already on a dead run, to be taken. The skirmish began. Students scattered. Church teens fought the officers. One girl had removed a shoe and repeatedly bashed Townsend in the head. Officers didn't return the blows, but fended them off. No weapons were ever drawn. These were kids, and no matter how they behaved the mission was to intervene with Lora Triplett. The lawmen were not going to allow her to escape.

Deputy Townsend forced his way through the angry mob of a dozen screaming youths—some being restrained by other officers. By the time he reached Lora, the girl wielding the shoe had gotten in a few more blows to Townsend's head. Another deputy seized her as Townsend grabbed Lora.

Lora fought furiously. Townsend wrestled her to the floor and cuffed her. She was still screaming as he lifted her, and, followed by her father, propelled her out the nearest door while the remaining officers held the other angry teens at bay.

With the battle between the officers and church members still raging in the hallway, Townsend and Triplett got Lora into Townsend's patrol car and off school grounds.

They drove directly to the Sierra Vista Substation where Lora's siblings were being held and took her inside.

Until Deputy Townsend heard the shocked gasp from Sergeant Loyce Guthrie as they entered the station, he hadn't been aware that he was covered in blood. He had several flowing wounds in his forehead from the beating he had taken by the girl's shoe. His shirt was soaked.

Back at the school, sheriff deputies and Sierra Vista Police Officers had subdued the angry teens. They took seven of them into custody.[7]

No teen had been injured. Lora Triplett's intervention had been successful. And the only one bleeding was Deputy Bill Townsend.

Debriefing

The four Triplett children were taken to a secret location—the Desert Inn on the west side of Tucson. Deputies Bill Townsend and Vince Madrid accompanied them. At the motel, Investigator John Barnes and several DPS officers met them. Barnes had secured the location. The DPS men were there to act as security. No one wore a uniform and no one was armed around the children.

In addition to the law enforcement personnel, there were two other men waiting. They were called "Dennis" and "Joe." Dennis and Joe were not their real names. They were professional deprogrammers, brought in from California by Sheriff Judd. Joe became a deprogrammer after a difficult experience with a family member who had once been in a draconian religious cult. Dennis had once been a cult member who had, himself, been deprogrammed years before. These were men who lived underground and did their difficult work with the constant awareness that they ran the risk of being arrested on kidnapping charges. That had never happened, and even though the risk was minimal, under these circumstances, they maintained their anonymity.

For the next several days, Dennis, Joe, Bill Townsend, and Vince Madrid spent hours with each of the children. The children were frightened and not forthcoming. Part of the mission was to ease the children into understanding that the real world was not as it had been represented to them by the church. The other part was to gain whatever real information they could about what was going on inside the cult.

The two younger ones had very little information about the cult, but they began to realize these were kind men who cared about their welfare and that maybe all white people weren't monsters.

Lora offered nothing. She refused to pay any attention to anything that was being said and spent almost all of her time on her knees clutching a Bible, with her face buried in a chair. The deprogrammers commented that these children were as controlled as any they had ever encountered.

But on the fourth day, Janet started to come around. Persistent gentle coaxing was having an affect. At first, all of her responses were what the professionals had expected: White people were the enemy; law enforcement wanted to kill them all; Mrs. Thomas was God; there were no weapons at the church.

When Lora was asked if William Thomas, Jr. was carrying a large handgun, she responded, "Brother William has no guns, nobody has any guns." That was clearly not the case. What other weapons he may have possessed cannot be known, although he had access to many that were bought by other church members.

According to ATF records of mandatory forms filled out at the time of purchase, William Thomas, Jr., on March 24, 1979, had purchased a .357 caliber stainless steel, Model Nineteen revolver at Sierra Vista Jewelers. On August 13, 1979, he bought a .30 caliber Universal Carbine and six thirty-round clips. The stainless steel revolver was apparently his favorite weapon. He was seen carrying it many times by many different people.

After another day, Janet began to relax, and the truth started coming out. Janet, only fourteen years old, had been one of the armed guards in God's Garage. She had been given a .38 revolver and—along with several others—spent many nights sitting up in Mrs. Thomas's garage or patrolling around the house, watching for white neighbors or deputies who could come at any time " to get them."

Janet told them that when Deputy Townsend and her father entered the church to serve the warrant to pick up the children, she had seen a churchwoman "load a thirty-eight gun" after they had been ushered into a back room. Janet recalled her saying, "I'm gonna kill that white boy."

During the sixth night at the Desert Inn, the DPS officer assigned to monitor the hallway fell asleep. While he slept, Janet crept from her room and joined her sister, Lora, in hers.

By morning, after a full night of counseling by Lora, Janet was again fully controlled. She was not communicating and terrified that the white men's real plan was eventually to kill her when they'd gotten what they wanted from her.

It took two more days of patient effort by Dennis before she calmed down and began speaking freely. They again convinced her of their good intentions. She was coming around, but had little more to offer about the cult. It was, however, from Janet that they learned the story of Steven Lindsey's funeral and Pastor Thomas's pronouncement that she had resurrected him.

By then, the church had hired an attorney and the court ordered the children be brought to Bisbee and allowed to be interviewed by him and Judge Lloyd C. Helm.

These interviews went on for several days, and the children went back and forth from Tucson to Bisbee.

The deputies and the deprogrammers gained nothing further from the children about the cult—but the three younger ones were no longer frightened of the men and were interacting positively with their father.

When Townsend and the children were not in court, but still in the Bisbee area awaiting another appearance, they stayed mobile, cruising remote areas to avoid an encounter with churchmen who may attempt to take the children back by force. In the meantime, Pastor Thomas and Willie Triplett had a conversation. According to

Willie, the pastor asked that he lie about his father —to say he hadn't ever been a father to him. When asked why he was asked to lie, Willie replied that "she didn't want the children taken away." Willie said his dad, Lester Triplett, was a good father.[8]

The following day, the court made its decision. Lester Triplett had the full right to keep his children. He was their legal guardian. The children were placed into their father's care and one day later, he returned with them to Mississippi.

Janet, Rusa Mae, and Robert stayed in Mississippi with Lester and other relatives. Three weeks later, Lora was back in Miracle Valley—retrieved by her sister Susie McCane.

Endnotes

[1] Arizona Daily Star, February 21, 1982.

[2] Arizona Daily Star, February 21, 1982.

[3] Arizona Daily Star, February 21, 1984.

[4] Triplett Deposition, October 11, 1984.

[5] Interview with Bill Townsend, April 26, 2006.

[6] Interview with Bill Townsend, April 26, 2006.

[7] Arizona Daily Star, January 12, 1982.

[8] Triplett Deposition , October 11, 1984.

Chapter Twenty

Melee at Buena

April 20, 1982

On April 19, 1982, CMHCC teens that were students at Buena High School clashed with white students in an alley behind the school. Punches were thrown, and both sides yelled racial epithets. A white woman who witnessed the incident was in the wrong place at the wrong time. She was knocked to the ground and reportedly kicked by church teen Ricky Brown.

Police were called. When they arrived, the black teens took off running, but officers caught Brown and arrested him for aggravated assault upon the woman. His arrest did not sit well with the church and, true to their history, they plotted revenge.

The following day, April twentieth, twenty church members—mostly teens and a few adults including William Thomas, Jr. and his brother Carl—arrived at the Buena campus. They were angry and entered school grounds looking for the white youths involved in the previous day's altercation. Fights began to erupt again. A female student was punched, fell and kicked in the face.

Sierra Vista Police and the sheriff were called and a dozen officers responded. Among those was Sergeant Loyce Guthrie, the first female deputy in the Cochise County Sheriff's Department. Sierra Vista Policeman Thomas Alinen was told to arrest church member Ricky Lamar for disorderly conduct.[1] It was easier said than done.

The lawmen confronted the church members and were almost immediately attacked. The lawmen were overwhelmed. The church teens and their adult companions threw punches, and several wielded clubs. SVPD officer Bob Randall held a female church member in a headlock as another tried to handcuff her. Suddenly a member of the mob relieved him of a nightstick and struck him in the face.[2] The officer stood unfazed for a moment, drew his weapon, and dropped to the ground, unconscious.

At least three officers were down and injured. The fight migrated onto Fry Boulevard, in front of the school, where it continued. One group of teens leapt into a car and streaked away. William Thomas, Jr. pulled his car onto Fry Boulevard and successfully blocked officers while another group of teens dragged a local couple from their car, dumped them on the street, leapt in, and sped away. Thomas, Jr. and his brother, in Thomas's black Lincoln, quickly followed them.

Officers took chase with lights flashing and sirens screaming. Church members hit speeds of one hundred miles per hour. Two roadblocks were put up—but not in time—and both were circum-navigated. The cars blasted down Highway Ninety-two, followed by the pursuing officers.

They made it to the church compound. By the time officers pulled up on the highway near the church, a mob of over one hundred adult church members had formed. They were angry and screaming. Dust still hung in the air. The cars were parked and empty.

The officers demanded that the church give up those involved. The angry crowd refused. It was a standoff. Sheriff Judd made the decision to have the officers stand down rather than precipitate a further, more violent confrontation.

The sheriff, armed with a list of fifteen named suspects, immediately met with County Attorney Beverly Jenny. The county attorney issued a search warrant detailing virtually every piece of property and vehicle owned by members of the church. The "Buena Fifteen" were secreted somewhere inside Miracle Valley, and the warrant would give the officials legal access to conduct a proper search. It was assumed the church would expect the sheriff to make an effort to arrest the church members involved. Reconnaissance by deputies confirmed increased activity, including the deployment of vehicles and men with weapons within the compound.

At that point, the sheriff's intention was to serve the warrant. Before proceeding, Sheriff Judd considered his limited resources. He was aware of the positive effect that a show of force had made previously. Judd contacted Ralph Milstead for support. The DPS Director's response was not what the sheriff had hoped for or expected.

Refrigerated Box Cars

In their conversation, Milstead—knowing Judd was one who always looked for a way to create peace above conflict—clearly did not want the sheriff to pursue the suspects. Milstead responded, "Your plan had better involve refrigerated box cars to hold all the bodies on both sides." He also indicated that Child Protective Services should be on hand for the orphaned children and that Judd should be prepared to provide counseling services for the widows of the church members and the deputies. "You are a reasonable man. You are a good sheriff. You are capable of making good decisions."

Milstead refused to send DPS support. He also believed he could influence Judd's decision—and he was right; suggesting instead that he (Milstead) come to town and play mediator. Milstead wanted himself and Judd to sit with Mrs. Thomas and her people and discuss the situation. He indicated that he would be able to convince her to relinquish the suspects.

The sheriff had been faced with a situation with very few ways of coming out ahead. There were fifteen people who had seriously broken the law. The sheriff had both the right and the obligation to go into Miracle Valley, search for, and apprehend them. The pressure from an angry white community who felt imprisoned was incredible. Deputies were becoming frustrated by years of easing off on what the sheriff had called, "wanton lawlessness."

Ever since Judd's first advisories from Ralph Milstead and Governor Babbitt, he'd been trying to keep a "lid on the situation" and avoid doing anything that might inflame it. The problem was the cult had moved past their ability or willingness to have any meaningful dialogue with the sheriff or his people—most definitely on the subject of giving up the fifteen teens.

Thunder Mountain

On April 27, Ralph Milstead arrived in Sierra Vista, and the negotiations began. Sheriff Jimmy Judd, Milstead, Pastor Frances Thomas, and Bishop William Thomas, Jr., (aka Field Marshal) met at the Thunder Mountain Inn, a motel on Highway Ninety-two on the outskirts of Sierra Vista.

The Sheriff's Personal Dilemma

The stress and responsibility that Sheriff Jimmy Judd felt in trying to manage a situation where he felt his hands were so often tied was huge. Important people were choosing to ignore the danger the CMHCC presented. The reality was clear for all to see—but ignored. The events were projecting themselves onto a national stage. Friends who knew the sheriff said, "Jimmy was not a happy man."

Beyond his responsibilities to his fellow lawmen, citizens, and even the church members was his responsibility to his family. Judd had a loving wife and five children that were directly feeling the consequences of his position. One of his daughters, Lyle remembers when a drive-by shooter pumped some shots into their St. David house one night. Most of the shots buried themselves in the exterior stucco. However, several shots crashed through a window and into the bedroom she shared with her sister Margo.[3]

In one assassination attempt, the sheriff was headed home. As he left Bisbee and passed through some low hills, a man rose up from the side of the road. The gunman let loose with a shotgun blast, blowing the drivers side rearview mirror and searchlight off his vehicle.

Sheriff Judd with his patrol car before leaving Bisbee. Photo courtesy of the Arizona Daily Star.

In addition there were a couple of bomb scares and numerous phone calls threatening to kill Judd and his family. In Phoenix, there was also a disturbing rumor—that someone was putting out a "hit" on Sheriff Judd.

They sat and negotiated for several days. Milstead offered compromises and the assurance that no harm would come to their teens. The two sides danced back and forth, but Frances Thomas had no intention of giving up the church members. She detested the sheriff. He had come to personify everything she hated about white people and stated she "was afraid the sheriff would beat or kill the children if [she] turned them over." Her son reminded the group, "Judd is Hitler." They were adamant.

The negotiations went nowhere. It was a stalemate at best. But while they sat at the Thunder Mountain Inn, another event was playing out in Miracle Valley that would have a vastly more dramatic impact.

Endnotes

[1] Interview of Officer Alinen, April 21, 1982 by SVPD Detective Bernheim, and DPS Agent Carl Kjellstrom.

[2] According to witness Joseph Brooks and other Buena High School students.

[3] Interview with Lyle (Judd) Acosta, August 23, 2008.

Chapter Twenty-one

Hammers and National News

April 29, 1982

As a result of the melee at Buena High School, two video crews from KOLD TV in Tucson were dispatched to take shots of Miracle Valley. A reporter was present to do a "stand-up" out on the highway. Mostly, their assignment was to get basic footage of the area and the church and anything else they were able to capture on tape while there. It should have been an easy assignment—a brief report and what the industry calls "B-Roll" or stock footage.

The reality turned out to be something quite different. Instead of capturing "B-Roll," one of the crews videotaped the other, and that footage became the object of local, national, and even international news.

KOLD reporter Barbara Morse was seated in the driver's seat of the compact station wagon that was parked on the north-side shoulder of Highway Ninety-two with the engine turned off. Cameraman Jamie Lopez was beginning to unload his gear. Across the road about thirty yards away, the second KOLD crew was already in place and caught on tape everything that happened next.

Five women church members—Gloria Tate, India Pipkins, Linda Pipkins, another Pipkins sister, and Jennifer Jones—pulled their car over on the south shoulder when they spotted the car with Morse and the cameraman. The five wandered casually over to the parked station wagon. The rear hatch was open.

Lopez struggled with the heavy recording deck hanging from his left shoulder and the video camera in his right hand. He managed to close the car hatch. He was a few feet away from the women when they began screaming.

Gloria Tate ran to the open passenger's side door, leaned in,

134

hammer raised as though she might strike, and ordered Morse to "give her the keys." Instead, Morse started the car and began moving forward. Tate staggered back as the car moved.

Barbara Morse moves the car forward. Notice church member with hammer (circled). DPS photo from video used for evidence.

The women ordered the cameraman away from the area. He didn't argue and ran for the moving car. As the women screamed insults and threats, three of them produced hammers they had hidden beneath their sweaters—they were regular carpenter's claw hammers, which were deadly weapons when thrown.

The cameraman, hauling the heavy video camera and external recording deck, dashed for the car. The screaming women hauled back and threw the hammers with all the strength they had. The cameraman ducked. Hammers bounced off the car. The women ran forward as the car moved. They picked up the hammers and threw again. The car stopped just long enough for Lopez to heave in the equipment and leap in behind it. As they sped away, the women had time for one last volley of hammers. The women were proud of their victory and laughed as they watched the station wagon speed away.

Women chase fleeing television cameraman. One woman gets ready to throw a hammer (circled) at him. DPS photo from video used for evidence.

The woman tosses a hammer (circled) that will sail over his head. The other women will bombard the vehicle with hammers as it drives off. DPS photo from video used for evidence.

This was precisely the kind of reception sheriff's deputies had become accustomed to. Others who had unwittingly stumbled into Miracle Valley typically received the same. While this encounter was no more violent than most, it differed in one very significant way. This encounter was on tape. The second crew had recorded the entire performance—in color and sound.

It was a vivid example of what Sheriff Judd called, "the lawlessness of the church," and it was now available for public scrutiny.

Television stations across the country ran the footage. The story went international. It ran for days. That much public attention that was focused on the situation and the area was bound to have an effect—and it did, in three significant ways.

First, the public finally had a viewable, audible, and very graphic example of precisely what the sheriff and his people had been tolerating for over two years.

Second, the church's bargaining power dropped significantly. Their national image as poor, peaceful people being persecuted by a redneck sheriff had been destroyed. Judd's assessment of the situation had become embarrassingly accurate.

And finally, for the first time, the governor got directly involved.

The Governor

The governor was in a politically embarrassing position. The discomforting situation of Miracle Valley—a situation he hoped would go away—was out of control.

With the hammer incident having become international news, the governor wasted no time getting involved. On April 29, Bruce Babbitt flew secretly to Sierra Vista to join the negotiations.[1]

Governor Babbitt claimed his interest in the matter was due to him wanting to bring the situation to a peaceful resolution, and, of course, wanting to rescue Arizona from the terrible international press coverage.

The cult and Pastor Thomas had been intransigent in their position about surrendering the Buena Fifteen. Now there had been a tipping point. Pastor Thomas was reconsidering her position, much to the displeasure of her more militant son. The pastor was looking for a way out.

The governor's meeting improved the stalemated situation. Babbitt spent the afternoon negotiating—knowing the pastor's clout was seriously diminished. He rightly surmised that Pastor Thomas would be willing to consider what the most powerful man in the state had to offer, more than the suggestions of anyone else.

Pastor Frances Thomas, despite the objections of her son, capitulated, and agreed to surrender the fifteen teens involved in the Buena High School melee.

The next day, Pastor Thomas and several other adult church members delivered the fifteen teens to the police station in Sierra Vista, and there the students stayed. Later, Thomas would claim her agreement with Governor Babbitt was that the teens would be held for no more than a few hours, then released.

Miscommunication

The students were held for several weeks. Pastor Thomas claimed she'd made an agreement with the governor, which was not met. Yet, she managed again to blame the sheriff. When confronted, Undersheriff Dale Lehman responded, "The county would never have agreed to anything like that." He meant that he couldn't speak for the state, but no matter what was discussed between the governor and the church, Cochise County was the local government's jurisdiction: "We did not and would never make such an agreement," Lehman announced.

Later, the governor would admit the possibility of the church members "inferring" only a few hours of detention. At the very least, any agreement made at the Thunder Mountain Inn between the church and the governor was pretty loose. Ironclad agreements leave no room for "inferring."

With official decisions, there is usually a line of text at which a finger can be pointed. There was none. But the state admitted the possibility of the church members "inferring." The question is why the governor would make a personal appearance, negotiate a deal firm enough to result in the turning over of the fifteen defendants, shake hands, return nods, and leave the decision open enough for the church members to "infer" anything.

Perhaps Mrs. Thomas, who was particularly adept at believing what she wished, simply created her own truth. Perhaps the governor left her the room to do so; but with all the power at his disposal, the governor elected to show a subtle weakness with these people who had continuously demonstrated their wanton disregard for authority. Pastor Thomas made a strategic withdrawal, but she would live to fight another day.

Sheriff Judd thanked the governor for his intervention. It did, after all, have a positive effect, and violence had been avoided. The sheriff had been faced with a situation with very few ways of coming out ahead. There were fifteen people who had broken the law. The sheriff had both the right and the obligation to go into Miracle Valley, search for, and apprehend them.

The pressure was incredible from an angry (non-CMHCC) community who felt imprisoned. Deputies were becoming frustrated by years of easing-off on what the sheriff rightly called wanton lawlessness. Ever since Judd's first advisory from Ralph Milstead, he'd been trying to keep a lid on things, rather than do anything that might further inflame the situation.

The governor came to town and sat down with all the parties and negotiated a temporary peace. Sheriff Judd congratulated the proceeding, saying, "Lives may have been saved by this wise and reasonable decision."

The church had lost much of its clout because of the hammer-throwing incident and its capitulation on the surrender of the Buena Fifteen. Mrs. Thomas could only be who she was. Everyone else heard gratitude for a peaceful settlement.

The bottom line was that the incident left room for all the parties concerned to make miscalculations—which in the end had deadly consequences.[2]

Endnotes

[1] Herald-Dispatch and Bisbee Review, May 29, 1983.

[2] The more immediate consequences of the Melee at Buena—which became known in the press as "The Buena Riot Case"—resulted in five people being formally charged. Of those, two were acquitted for lack of evidence. A five-year sentence for armed robbery was meted out to Ricky Brown. Lonnie Hayes received three and a half years for aggravated assault; and Ricky Lamar got thirty days for committing assault on a law enforcement officer. Of the five women charged with aggravated assault in the hammer throwing incident, three were acquitted. Gloria Tate and India Pipkins received probation for misdemeanor assault.

Chapter Twenty-two

The Night Before

October 22, 1982

Sheriff Judd had placated the cult and done everything possible to improve every situation in an unsuccessful effort to maintain peace in Miracle Valley. Too many times he had heard the words, "your laws don't apply to us." But even with mountains of provocation, he was still a man who wanted only peace in his jurisdiction.[1] Many of his deputies over the past two years had pressured the sheriff to take action—to go in and deal with the group who continually and so blatantly flaunted the law.

Deputies frustrated with "keeping the lid on" had been eager to take a more active approach to the problem. A number of lawmen, including Captain Goodman, had wanted to make a show of force to cause the cult members to recognize that their reign of terror and intimidation was over. The church still had that opportunity to live in peace in Cochise County. But many in the department believed it was a very real option to force the militant church members to recognize that the sheriff was prepared to solve the problem by any means necessary.

The sheriff had, in fact, reached the point of deciding to make that necessary show of force on several occasions. During the previous year, deputies had received a "call out" twice, and twice had been ordered to stand-down. The sheriff was prepared to take action, but had been convinced by DPS Director Milstead or Governor Babbitt to hold off.

Repeatedly, Sheriff Judd had sought and received advice from Director Milstead or Governor Babbitt, whom he believed spoke in the best interests of peace—always advising a hands-off posture. Advice he accepted, even when Judd's instincts advised him differently. He believed these were honorable men with greater experience in matters such as these, and never questioned their motives—in hindsight, Sheriff Judd probably needed to be questioning their motives.

There had been problems after the Buena Riot and the hammer-throwing incident, but for most of the next five months, there had been a lull. Perhaps Pastor Thomas and her flock were regrouping. Perhaps there was a power struggle occurring between Pastor Thomas and her son, William.

Pastor Thomas's response to her retreat after the Buena Riot fiasco was legal. She filed a seventy-five million dollar lawsuit on June 11, 1982, in the US District Court in Tucson. The suit charged violations of the Civil Rights Act by various Cochise County officials (including Sheriff Judd).[2]

Among the components of the suit were: two shows of force; the Triplett affair; traffic stops for harassment purposes; the Drew investigation; and detaining juveniles (after the Buena High School riot).[3]

It is known that there were increasing financial pressures on the cult. Pastor Thomas had brought a suit against Cochise County and Sheriff Judd—perhaps legal bills were draining funds from the cult. It was rumored the Pastor Thomas's CMHCC was three hundred thousand dollars in debt.

After the events of October 23, 1982, another item would be added to the lawsuit.

Escalation: October 22, 1982 (night)

During the previous week, encounters between cult members and deputies had escalated. Church members had again become convinced they were untouchable—that their leaders were correct when they said, "The white man's law doesn't apply to us."

It had become commonplace for church members to flee a pursuing sheriff's or DPS vehicle—only to have the officer break off the pursuit, rather than enter the compound area where they were almost certain to find a violent reception.

On the night of Friday, October 22, two significant events occurred that set in motion a process that would become a deadly encounter.

It was after dark when Deputies Brad Geeck and Jeff Brown

(a rookie) went into Miracle Valley to serve the warrant on Frank Bernard. They didn't make it very far into the compound before angry cult members—fifteen to twenty of them, all armed in some way—overwhelmed the deputies. Some members had firearms, others a variety of clubs. They clearly saw law enforcement, no matter how it was defined, as the enemy; and no warrants were going to be served now or ever upon their brethren.

It was immediately apparent to the deputies that they had entered a life-threatening situation. Screaming, armed people vastly outnumbered the lawmen. The mob believed they were above any law the deputies represented. Finding Frank Bernard was no longer the issue. The deputies' only concern was getting out alive—and that they did. Little did Deputy Brown know it, but he would face the same situation in less than twenty-four hours.

The deputies' report to Sheriff Judd that evening became the final straw. The time for tolerance was over. The time for action had arrived.

A Time for Action

Bench warrants had been issued for church member Frank Bernard and two other churchmen for multiple non-appearances in court for many moving traffic violations. These were not traffic tickets—they were arrest warrants. This was no longer something the sheriff could find tolerable. The church had run roughshod over the community for years. His patience had come to an end, and he called DPS.

Director Ralph Milstead had carried Babbitt's messages of avoiding confrontation in Miracle Valley to the sheriff many times; so far Judd had accepted the advice. It was apparently the governor's hope that Milstead could once again convince the sheriff to put away his concerns and allow the church to continue behaving in whatever way it pleased—unmolested by the Cochise County Sheriff.

But the sheriff could no longer accept that he nor any other responsible officer of the law could allow this behavior to continue. Sheriff Judd told Milstead that he and his men were finally forced into a position of dealing with the situation.

He also reminded Director Milstead of his and the governor's promises of support if and when the time ever came for such action. For the first time, the sheriff did not back off at Milstead's request. Judd let Director Milstead know that while he truly did not expect significant trouble—since his people should be able to create a reasonable enough show of force to forestall any serious retaliation by the church—he would still be counting on their support if it became necessary.

By the time he got off the phone, it is reported Milstead promised he would have DPS personnel assemble in Sierra Vista, and if called, they would be ready.

The Element of Surprise

One thing the sheriff knew was in his favor was the element of surprise. The church people would have no idea that Judd's men would arrive in the morning to serve Bernard's warrant. They should be able to go in, get Frank Bernard, and be out with a minimum of difficulty. He would have his force in readiness; however, if they should be needed. Judd then went about the process of alerting his key people—Captain Goodman, Sergeant Barnett, and Sergeant Dever. They, in turn, notified their subordinates that they should arrive at the Bisbee headquarters first thing in the morning. It was time to make a plan for action.

It was then that Sheriff Judd got wind that an article about the aborted arrest attempt by Deputies Brown and Geeck was scheduled to appear in the next edition of the *Tucson Citizen* Newspaper. He became concerned it might inflame the church members. Judd called the paper's City Editor David McCumber and asked that he not run, or at least hold off on, publishing the article.

It was the sheriff's call to McCumber that became the second significant event. It triggered a series of phone calls, beginning with one said to be placed by McCumber to Governor Bruce Babbitt, alerting him to the possibility of things coming to a head between the sheriff's department and the cult. The governor, in turn, placed a call to DPS Director Ralph Milstead. Milstead informed him of Judd's decision to do what he had to do to maintain order in his jurisdiction. Presumably, Milstead reported the conversation he had with Judd earlier and his promise of support. Whether or not Babbitt vetoed the DPS promise of support at this point is a matter of conjecture.

The final call to the sheriff came from Babbitt himself. His minion

Milstead had been unsuccessful in getting Judd to back away from his sworn duty. Perhaps the governor might be more successful. Babbitt "begged Jimmy Judd not to go serve the warrants." He pleaded with the sheriff "to negotiate, to call [Mrs. Thomas's] lawyers." Judd replied that the warrants were going to be served—he would enforce law equally in Cochise County.[4]

Judd assured Babbitt that he would not do anything to overtly agitate the situation, but that the church members were not so far above the law as they believed, and the outstanding warrants would be served. Before the call ended, the sheriff reminded Babbitt of his promise of support if the situation ever called for additional backup— while no one could predict the outcome of the warrants being served, the time had come to call in that promise.

This is the point at which Sheriff Judd could safely assume that any further calls from or between Babbitt and Milstead would be to organize the support that they had always promised. Clearly such calls were made, as was evidenced by the increased DPS build-up in Sierra Vista. DPS officers were being deployed.

However, unbeknownst to Sheriff Judd, his assumption was anything but safe.

An Informer

Another call was made. If Judd had known about this call, he probably would have altered—and very probably halted—his plan. Harold Hurtt, "the governor's mediator," had been used regularly as a liaison between the governor and the cult. Either the governor or Ralph Milstead contacted him. It would have been odd if Milstead had contacted Hurtt without being directed to do so by Babbitt.

In any event, Hurtt was told about the sheriff's intentions. The call he made next may easily have been the tipping point in what was to become known as "the Shootout at Miracle Valley."

Hurtt's apparent call was one that to this day both shocks and baffles everyone involved. It was an action that people in law enforcement do not do to each other. Harold Hurtt called the church and told them the sheriff was coming.[5]

Endnotes

[1] During a March 8, 2008 interview Buddy Hale recalls how Pastor Thomas, Sheriff Judd and a DPS official met in A. A. Allen's old Bible College in late September of 1982. They tried to negotiate the execution of fifteen outstanding warrants. During the meeting the Pastor's rhetoric was considerably more strident. Again and again she told them that "your law doesn't apply in Miracle Valley" and that Miracle Valley "belonged to her." She relented at last, but when an attempt to serve the warrants was made the next night by Hale and several deputies the results were the same or worse. Their cars were blocked in and they faced forty men—many with rifles and shoulder holsters. Hale told his men to abandon their cars if shooting started. Finally, William Thomas, Jr. arrived and allowed them to leave.

[2] Sacks, Status Report CIV 82-343 TUC ACM.

[3] Sacks, Status Report CIV 82-343 TUC ACM.

[4] As related by Sheriff Judd to Larry Dempster, Bert Goodman and others.

[5] According to an article in the 11-17-82 Herald-Dispatch and Bisbee Review, Judd reported Harold Hurtt talked to Pastor Thomas before the bloody encounter.

Chapter Twenty-three

Final Plans

Oct 23, 1982—12:00 AM

The midnight oil was burning at the Cochise County Sheriff's Department. Sheriff Judd, County Attorney Beverly Jenny, Bill Breen from ACISA, and Judd's senior staff were busy. The sheriff had made the decision to serve the arrest warrants on Frank Bernard and two other church members. The department was on alert, and a meeting with all individuals involved had been scheduled for later in the morning.

A little after midnight, Sheriff Judd and Undersheriff Dale Lehman met with Captain Bert Goodman to discuss a plan. Judd's close friend, Bert Goodman, would be in charge.

Addressing Goodman, the sheriff asked, "So, how do you want to handle this, Bert?"

Goodman already had a plan: "I'll go in with one other man. One car—minimum threat. Have backup down the road if we need them."

Undersheriff Lehman offered the possibility of going in full force. The sheriff said no. They'd stick with Bert's plan, and for the next hour, the men laid out the deployment of personnel.

It was the sheriff's assumption that if there was any resistance, his staged deputies could make a show-of-force sufficient to diffuse the situation. If Captain Goodman was met with enough resistance to keep him from serving the warrants, the department would be prepared to send in as few or as many cars as necessary to take care of the situation. The sheriff also had the promise of an equal force of DPS officers, who would be staged and ready to supply support if needed.

Based on years of witnessing their behavior patterns, the sheriff made a safe assumption that the cult members would be loud and make attempts at intimidating his men. The sheriff also knew that the cult members had always backed off in the past and that his force was ready in sufficient numbers. And as a trump card, Judd had the guarantee of DPS support. The sheriff was confident warrants could be served and the men could be taken into custody without anything approaching violence.

Finally, the sheriff knew he had the element of surprise on his side—which he considered the critical centerpiece of his strategy.

Goodman should be able to enter the area, confront Frank Bernard (at least, and hopefully all three men) with the warrants, and take them quietly into custody. With any luck, the officers would be out of the valley before the cult members were fully aware what was happening. The time had come to end the church's reign of terror in Miracle Valley.

The flaw, of course, was that Sheriff Judd was no longer in possession of the element of surprise. The members of the Christ Miracle Healing Center and Church had been warned, and they were on high alert. It has been reported, during the earlier call from Harold Hurtt, Pastor Frances Thomas made the statement, "If they come, none of them will leave this valley alive."[1] Whether or not she intended to make good on that threat, she was certainly prepared. Armed church members took up "ambush positions" throughout the compound, which they maintained throughout the night.

October 23, 6:30 AM—The Morning Meeting

The law enforcement group started arriving after 6:00 AM at the Bisbee headquarters. By 6:30 AM, the meeting had started. Sheriff Judd explained what had occurred the night before to Deputies Brown and Geeck. Then Lieutenant Craig Emanuel and Captain Bert Goodman described the plan that they and the sheriff had devised.

Captain Goodman, partnered with Deputy Pat Halloran, would go into the church compound alone in one car. They would carry arrest warrants for Frank Bernard and two others.

They expected some bluster and threatening, but they had surprise on their side. The sheriff believed the two deputies could probably extract the suspects (at least Bernard) and leave without a serious conflict. But to make the assumption that nothing more serious might occur would be foolhardy, especially after all the previous violent encounters they'd had with church members. Fortunately, experience had taught that, in every case, a reasonable show of force had caused the church members to back down.

Goodman explained how he and Halloran would go in alone, but if necessary, the full force of the department would be in position to go in as backup if needed.[2]

Thirty-five deputies would be deployed in seventeen cars. Half of them would stay on Kings Ranch Road—about two miles to the west of the valley—and the others would stay near the fire station on Palominas Road—about two miles away to the east. There they would wait until they were called. Captain Goodman would be in charge of the operation.

Lieutenant Craig Emanuel made the assignments. Among them, Deputy Ray Thatcher was teamed with Deputy Dave Jark. Thatcher, in addition to his regular duties as a patrolling deputy, was the designated sniper on the department's SWAT team, which was lead by Sergeant Larry Dever.

Deputy Thatcher had been well trained for the assignment for almost a year. Thatcher was a crack shot who constantly practiced with various weapons. Among those weapons was the Ruger Mini-Fourteen, which was the weapon he would carry that day. The Ruger was intended to be fired from the shoulder as a sniper rifle. In addition to practicing firing the weapon as a sniper rifle, Thatcher also spent hours and thousands of rounds of ammunition practicing firing the Ruger from the hip. Deputy Jark would be there to back him up.

Thatcher and Jark would be in the last car in the procession along Kings Ranch Road. If these deputies were called into the valley, they would take up a position on the far perimeter of the compound. Thatcher was the sniper. His job would be to "take out" armed aggressors from a distance. No one thought he would have to make use of his practice..

It was originally the sheriff's plan to go in himself, but he became convinced by his men that it was not a good idea. The sheriff was the primary focus of Mrs. Thomas's anger and hatred of all things white and legal. His presence promised to do nothing but inflame a situation that should otherwise go relatively smoothly. Judd could not fight that logic and agreed to remain at his command post, monitoring the radio and issuing orders as necessary.

Judd ended the meeting by telling his deputies that if any of them did not want to go, they did not have to. There would be no hard feelings. Two deputies declined to go because of their age.

Shortly after seven o'clock the deputies left the Sheriff's office. They were quiet as they headed to their vehicles. While not one soul was eager for an all-out confrontation, anything could happen and they were prepared—or so they believed.

Had the sheriff known the cult had been tipped off, he would have ended the operation before it began. "Had I known, we would never have gone in," the sheriff later remarked.

Endnotes

[1] Again, according to an article in the November 17, 1982 Herald-Dispatch and Bisbee Review, Judd reported Harold Hurtt talked to Pastor Thomas before the bloody encounter. It is during this call that Judd says Pastor Thomas made her threat.

[2] During a 1981 radio interview Sheriff Judd noted that despite the difficulties with Pastor Thomas his budget and staff to patrol Cochise County had remained almost stable. At that time the number of officers in the Sheriff's department was about sixty or sixty-two. About half this number of personnel was available as backup on October 23, 1982.

Chapter Twenty-four

The Shootout at Miracle Valley

Deployment

The temperature is somewhere in the middle sixties, and it is slowly climbing. The sky is clear with just a few wispy clouds. To the east was the long-tolerated streak of smoke—looking like a fat jet contrail—that blows from the south to the north from a copper smelter, fifty miles below the border in Mexico.

Seventeen cars with thirty-five deputies are divided between Palominas Road on the west and Kings Ranch Road to the east, both several miles from the Miracle Valley compound. And there they wait for the call everyone hopes will never come.

As the deputies wait by their vehicles, some are apprehensive, but others are not particularly concerned. After all, every time the county or state has made a show of force, the cult reacts peacefully. Most officers don't expect to be sent in, nor do they think that a major confrontation will take place. They consider themselves backup.

Goodman & Halloran

Captain Bert Goodman and Pat Halloran wait in their marked vehicle a few miles down from Miracle Valley on Highway Ninety-two, until all of the other units are in place along Kings Ranch and Palominas Roads. They receive the radio call that everyone is in place, and they start to move.

At about 7:40 AM, Goodman and Halloran roll slowly into Miracle Valley. It is quiet and appears almost deserted.

Halloran stands by the car, while Goodman, warrants in hand, goes to the door of the house they know is occupied by Frank Bernard. He knocks and waits. The only response is quiet. Goodman announces his presence—still nothing. He tries the door, but it is locked. He looks in a couple of windows and sees only empty rooms.

It is still strangely quiet as Goodman moves on to the second house on his itinerary. It belongs to William Thomas, Jr. Again, he knocks, and the door swings open a few inches. He calls into the house, "I have a warrant!"

There is still nothing but an uncharacteristic silence.

He swings the door open and looks inside. It appears empty. He cautiously enters and looks around. There is no one there.

As he moves toward the third house on his list, faces begin to appear. A few people start milling around, watching. By the time he knocks on the next door, more church members are emerging from houses.

Bert Goodman is still on the porch of the third house when a burgundy Buick roars up and screeches to a skidding stop. Many, many faces are appearing from everywhere. The driver of the Buick leaps out brandishing a four-foot pipe. Two men in the rear of the car are holding long-barreled rifles or shotguns, and start to move. The growing crowd begins yelling; many are armed.

'The driver rushes at Goodman, hollering and beginning to wave the pipe back and forth, two inches from Goodman's face—close enough for Bert to feel the wind. The man is clearly trying to provoke violent action. Goodman keeps his arms folded across his chest while he dodges to keep from being hit by the pipe. It is turning into a life and death game of chicken. Bert Goodman knows if he draws his weapon, he'll be cut in half before his gun clears the holster.

The crowd is becoming more agitated as the man continues to swing the pipe. Bert hears someone yell, "Shoot the guy in the cowboy hat!" Goodman thinks, "I'm the only one wearing a cowboy hat." Adrenaline is pumping, but Goodman knows he has to "damn well" resist the urge to draw his weapon.[1]

Suddenly, Halloran races in and grabs the pipe away from the screaming man and pauses—the crowd is taken by surprise. Halloran and Goodman cuff the assailant and wrestle him toward their car. They toss him in the back and slam the door.

Halloran reaches in the vehicle and grabs the radio mike. "Meeting resistance."

The crowd recovers from their surprise and roar. They are everywhere. Two seconds later, Halloran radios again, "Having confrontations."

Goodman yells to Halloran, "Call for backup."

"Send one!"

The response comes back, "Define."

"Send one car!"

Goodman yells, "Send two!'"

Halloran repeats the order, "Send two!"

The mob is going wild. Weapons are appearing. Guns start poking out of windows. Goodman shouts again, "Send them all!" Halloran relays his captain's order into the mike.

It isn't what they expected. It is the last thing anybody wanted. But the officers are being attacked and shots have been fired. Violence is breaking out in Miracle Valley.

By the time the backup units race into the fields, without lights or sirens to minimize any alert of their approach, there are over one hundred angry church members waiting to greet them—and the number is growing.

The church members had been warned the sheriff was coming, but didn't know when. Many of them had been up most of the night armed and ready, but some had retired after dawn when nobody appeared. They now re-emerge in force!

It is an area of two open fields surrounded with scattered houses and dirt roads. Each car takes up an available position in a field or along a road. Angry church members are everywhere—and every one of them believes themselves to be a "soldier of the Lord." Field Marshal William Thomas, Jr. has his commandos for Christ at his disposal.

Conflicts break out simultaneously across the open fields. As officers emerge from their vehicles, they are immediately bombarded by groups wielding pipes, rebar, rakes, two by fours, knives and in many cases, firearms. Church members who have already inflicted severe damage upon one deputy or another, move quickly to attack others.

Fletcher, Ebner, Self, Rutherford and Tomlinson

Bert Goodman and Pat Halloran continue fending off attackers. As they struggle against increasing odds, their prisoner starts to kick the back window out of the patrol car. After a concrete block sails through the window, the cuffed man escapes.

Among the first deputies on the scene is Jim Self. He is instantly set upon by three or four women. A woman attacks him with a rake. He wields a baton and snaps the rake in half. The woman retreats to find another weapon.

Self then sees a teenage boy race from one of the nearby houses waving a revolver and firing wildly at Captain Goodman—three, four, five, six shots ring out![2] It is too crowded to return fire. The boy disappears as Self is engulfed by attackers.

Lieutenant Homer Fletcher and Deputies Chuck Ebner and Mike Rutherford exit their car. They also are immediately overwhelmed. Church member Cornelius Hangar threatens them with a shotgun as another man (either Gus Gillespie or Otis Thompson—it was never definitely determined which) moves in wielding a metal pipe.

Deputy Chuck Ebner wrestles one man to the ground. Ebner cuffs him while being beaten by other church members. He still manages to haul the man to his vehicle. As Rutherford fends off his own attackers, Fletcher is taking repeated blows from the man wielding the metal pipe. One blow catches him on the neck below the protection of his helmet, and he goes down—out cold.

When Fletcher comes to, he is on his feet, being held up by two churchmen. A screaming churchwoman is directly in front of him, slashing at him with a broken Pepsi bottle. He is bleeding from a severe cut on his left shoulder and another on the right side of his waist below the area covered by his sleeveless vest, which has been nearly shredded by six more deep cuts.

As Fletcher wrestles himself into consciousness, several other deputies catch sight of his plight and move in to assist. When the woman and the men holding him see the deputies approaching, they abandon Fletcher and disappear into the melee.

The capitulation of those specific assailants hasn't ended Fletcher's, Ebner's, or Rutherford's involvement. The woman and men vanish into the crowd, and the rescuing deputies return to fending off their own attackers. Immediately, other church members fall upon them, fighting with a mindless fury.

By now, almost all the deputies are out of their cars and involved in confrontations in every section of the compound—all faced with overwhelming force. Thirty-five officers are pitted against at least one hundred and fifty furious church members—and yet the officers hold their fire. Men, women, and children crush in on them, all armed in one way or another.

Deputy Al Tomlinson meets one of the children face to face. He turns to see a twelve-year old boy rushing toward him with a .22 revolver. Tomlinson draws his service weapon and the boy stops. They stare at each other for a frozen moment. Tomlinson yells, "Get out of here!" The boy lowers his gun and flees.[3]

Shots whistle above the sheriff's men. As officers fight for their lives, many are surprised that church members aren't being hit by the cult members' own gunfire.

The Radio Room

Sheriff Jimmy Judd, County Attorney Beverly Jenny, Undersheriff Dale Lehman, Bill Breen of ACISA and a dispatcher are in the radio room of the Cochise County Sheriff's Department—listening. There is a single small slit of a window at the top of one wall. The group monitors the radio traffic from Miracle Valley. The frantic calls are mixed with gunshots and screaming—followed by the complete silence of the tiny room. More calls and more silence. Time slows to a crawl as the drama unfolds. Judd, Jenny, Lehman and Breen are overwhelmed with a sense of helplessness—and a need to be there. Bill Breen turns away and looks up at the single window.[4] He folds his hands and prays. He knows he can not respond to the chaos. Judd leaves for Miracle Valley.

Townsend and Madrid

Through the windshield, Deputies Bill Townsend and Vince Madrid can see other deputies in various battles. They bail out of their vehicle and charge forward to assist Guthrie, the only female deputy on scene. She is alone, surrounded, and fending off a vicious attack. Guthrie's arms and shoulders are bruised and bleeding from the assaults.

Townsend and Madrid are racing to her aid, but they don't make it fifteen feet before they are engaged in battles of their own. A big man runs toward Bill, yelling, "Get out of my way." Townsend holds his ground. The screaming man charges forward. Before the deputy can react, the man bashes him in the face. Townsend returns several blows, which rock the man back. As he moves toward his assailant, Townsend sees more men and women coming at him from the right.

Townsend doesn't see the woman come in from the left, wielding a two by four. She smashes him in the knees, but through the pain, he manages to remain standing. Then a blur of motion catches his attention. As he turns, a large rock hurled by another woman flies at him! It seems to come at him in slow motion, turning—as if it would take forever to reach him. Smash! It is fast enough to catch him in the left shoulder, below the protection of his sleeveless vest.

As he recoils from the blow, the first woman comes at him again with the two by four, swinging wildly, catching him squarely— tearing a piece of flesh out of his upper arm. Bill Townsend is separated from his partner by ten to fifteen yards. Madrid is fighting off several church members. They are screaming, throwing punches, and kicking. One man is right in front of Madrid—pushing and hollering. Madrid notices unidentified movement coming at him from above and from the left.

Vince instinctively holds up his left arm in defense. Otis Thompson delivers a crushing blow with a four-foot rebar to Madrid's arm, shattering the bone. Before he goes down, Deputy Madrid manages to hit Thompson once with his right fist. But it isn't enough to take Thompson out. As the injured Madrid tries to swing again, the rebar delivers another savage blow to his right hand, shattering more bone.

Madrid yells to his partner, "Bill, I'm down."

Fighting through his own pain, Townsend frees himself from his attackers and runs to aid Madrid. His partner is on the ground with a broken bone sticking out through his torn shirt; he is gushing blood, and the knuckles of his right hand are destroyed. A man runs up behind Townsend and throws a rock. It misses. Townsend turns on him and the man flees into the crowd.

Townsend, a formidable man, now only vaguely aware of the pain in his knees and arms, lifts the bleeding, severely injured Vince Madrid and carries him to their nearby vehicle. As they race out of the field, Townsend keys his radio mike and yells, "Officer down! Officer down! Enroute to Bisbee hospital."

Madrid is the first to be so terribly damaged that day. He will certainly not be the last. And yet, in order not to endanger the church members, all the deputies at this point consistently refrain from firing on the mob—even though random shots are being sporadically fired on them from the perimeter of the battlefield. It is a madhouse, but the deputies have not gone mad.

Rick Tutor, Buddy Hale and Jeff Brown

The battlefield consists of isolated groups or single deputies that are fighting for their lives. The CCSO car containing Sergeant Buddy Hale, Rick Tutor, Paul Gruen, and Jeff Brown pulls off Loaves and Fishes Road near Second Street. South of them, Pat Halloran and Captain Goodman are warding off blows and making a futile last plea for sanity. People continue to gather from everywhere.

As Hale and his men exit their vehicle, they can see a large group of men and women moving toward them. Rick Tutor leans forward in the back seat to retrieve his fiberglass nightstick. The back doors to the patrol car close and he is locked inside.[5] Since the back doors of a squad car can't be opened from the inside, Tutor kicks at a window to free himself. Gruen sees Tutor out of the corner of his eye and lets him out. The deputies form a semi-circle around the back of Hale's car.

A woman rushes forward to engage Deputy Tutor with an iron rake. She smashes the rake across his hand as he tries to deflect it with his nightstick. The fingers on his hand are crushed, but he doesn't notice. Tutor can't force himself to hit her. She continues her attacks and then disappears into the crowd.

Church member Ricky Lamar rushes at Hale. Lamar shoves him. Hale declares, "You're under arrest," and takes him down with the help of Tutor. Hale succeeds in getting one cuff on Ricky Lamar as they are engulfed in a wave of church members. Lamar retreats a few yards and pulls a large two by four out of the long brown grass.

Sergeant Hale disengages himself from his attackers and faces the onrushing threat. Deputy Jeff Brown steps in to help.

"Put it down, Ricky!" demands Brown.

"You know him?" Hale asks.

"Yeah, it's Ricky Lamar."

Ricky swings, but misses. Hale and Brown take the enraged man down and struggle to get the other cuff on the kicking and screaming Lamar. A group of men and women pull Sergeant Hale away and start beating him.

Jeff Brown is fully engaged with a wild Ricky Lamar. Lamar is on his feet, swinging at Deputy Brown with the two by four. Though fighting his own battle for survival, Hale can hear Lamar grunting as blow after blow descends on Deputy Jeff Brown. Again, Hale breaks free to help the twenty-seven year old Brown. Lamar flees the two deputies who turn and face an onrushing tsunami of attackers.

The two lawmen are buried under a group of fourteen or fifteen church members. George Gillespie sees Deputy Hale's legs extending out from beneath the "dog pile." He repeatedly jumps on Hale's legs—ripping the ligaments loose from the knees.[6]

Sergeant Hale struggles to his feet and is shoved back and onto the trunk of his car. A woman grabs Hale's nightstick and beats him with it. George Gillespie's brother Gus yells for the attackers to, "Break his arms! Break his arms!"

Hale realizes that if he is going home tonight, he has to do something. He starts gouging his attackers in the eyes and fights his way off the trunk of his car with the help of Deputy Brad Geeck.

Hale and Geeck immediately start receiving small-arms fire from trees to the north. A bullet lodges itself in the boot heel of Deputy Rick Tutor. Tutor is fighting a man swinging a baseball bat at him. The young deputy is being driven back as he attempts to ward of the blows. Tutor's nightstick bends almost into a "u" shape from the blows. As Tutor steps back he almost trips over a pick handle.[7] He grasps the pick handle and subdues his attacker. The man is pulled away in handcuffs.

In another part of the battlefield, Bishop Thomas drives up in another car. Men jump out of the vehicle and the Bishop pulls guns out of the trunk. The sounds of gunfire, the deputy's voices, and the screaming church members intermingle, indistinguishable from one another.

Deputy Tutor fights on. Despite the screams and gunfire it is a silent world to him—a world of protecting himself against blows and trying to subdue attackers. Silent until he hears rapid gunfire from a semi-automatic weapon. His hearing is restored. He reaches to draw his weapon and for the first time realizes his fingers are broken.

Deputy Jeff Brown's future dies in the dusty fields of Miracle Valley. The young deputy continues to fight, unaware that the blows supposedly inflicted by Ricky Lamar will end his life. The damage inflicted upon Brown will keep him in medical treatment for the next month. Many deputies will require medical attention, some for years or even decades to come—but for Jeff Brown his ordeal will end just thirty days later, when he succumbs to the wounds he suffers on the Miracle Valley battlefield. While many deputies are seriously injured, miraculously the rookie deputy is the only law enforcement officer destined to die as a result of the battle.

Rothrock, Guthrie, and Smith

Sergeant Loyce Guthrie is being bashed with rocks and by a screaming woman wielding a two by four. Guthrie is over six feet tall and solid. She is as capable as any man there, but every bit as vulnerable and taking beatings from all sides. She is engulfed by the mob and sustaining significant physical damage.

The deputies are each involved in their own battle, unable to render aid to each other. No sooner has Otis Thompson finished destroying Vince Madrid's arm and hand, than he moves swiftly to attack Rod Rothrock. Other rioters back away, giving Thompson room to swing the blood-covered rebar at Deputy Rothrock.

None have real riot gear. The deputies wear only helmets and vests and carry only nightsticks and side arms, which Captain Goodman has referred to as "six-round peashooters."

Rothrock is one of the only two deputies on scene with a PR-24 aluminum side-handle baton, with which he has been very well trained. Thompson rains blow after blow with the rebar at Rothrock, but they are fended off with the deputy's baton. Each rebuff sends painful vibrations up Rothrock's arms. Thompson leaps out of the way, narrowly escaping being hit by the baton—and realizing he is badly outclassed, Thompson backs off.

With battles raging all around him, Rothrock charges down the nearest road to assist other deputies, but is confronted no more than twenty yards from where he started by a young black man spinning numbchucks. It is churchman Robert Luckett, who has been seen many times over the years by non-church residents of the valley practicing with that and other weapons. Weapons training was demanded and expected by William Thomas, Jr. of all of his Commandos for Christ.

Numbchucks (constructed of two heavy wooden sticks connected at the top with a short chain) are deadly in the hands of a skilled practitioner. Robert Luckett is trained in the use of the deadly oriental weapon as well as Rothrock is trained with the baton.

As Luckett advances, Rothrock knows his baton is no match for the spinning numbchucks. He steps back and draws his sidearm, a .38 Smith and Wesson. Luckett is enraged, but he isn't stupid. He is now outmatched. At the sight of Rothrock's .38, he screams a parting epithet and vanishes into the melee.

With fighting all around him, Rothrock re-holsters his sidearm and is almost instantly opposed by a group of women—charging at him like angry bulls—throwing large rocks. A rock catches him painfully in the left thigh.

As the large deputy defends himself, another girl catches his attention—she has her hands cuffed behind her. She has obviously broken free from another deputy. She makes the mistake of moving in too close and Rothrock grabs her. Rothrock shoves an arm between her arms and back, and he starts hauling her toward a patrol car.

Twenty women converge, armed with rocks and screaming at Rothrock to release the girl. With his left arm, laced between the girl's arms, he continues to propel her toward the car. Two women rush up from behind. They began to furiously kick the deputy and beat at him with closed fists. After several more steps, Rothrock spins the girl around, using her as a shield.

Dever and Jones

Sergeant Larry Dever and Deputy Dave Jones race in, stopping their black Chevy Blazer in a spot near the northeast corner of the field. Sergeant Dever watches a car pull up behind him, in an attempt to block his escape route if needed. Dever exits and sees a man get out of the blocking car—with a rifle. He also notices that behind the man there are some people in a nearby yard, watching the melee. Sergeant Dever realizes he doesn't have a safe shot if he needs to use his sidearm. The man walks toward him, eyes directly ahead.

"Put down the rifle," orders Dever.

The man does not respond, but continues to walk toward him.

"Put down the weapon!" Dever shouts. There is no response— but to Dever's relief, the man walks past him. Dever turns and leans into the open door of the Blazer. A still-seated Deputy Jones and Dever reach into the back seat for rifles.

With Dever and Jones still in the process of grabbing their weapons, a maroon, white-topped Pontiac, owned by William Thomas, Jr. and used as a regular security patrol vehicle, skids to a stop nearby.

Deputy Rothrock is only twenty yards from Dever and Jones's vehicle. He is still hanging onto the thrashing, cuffed girl, when he spots two men leaping from the maroon car. They are both carrying long guns. He begins shouting: "Guys to the north have guns! Guns to the north!"

Dave Jones has not yet exited the Blazer. Dever is half-seated in the driver's seat and is in the process of yanking his rifle from the back seat. Jones spots the Pontiac at the same time as Rothrock and yells, "They're getting guns!" The "pop pop" of small-arms fire from the perimeter of the battlefield continues.

The activity is loud and frenetic; deputies are yelling about men with guns. The battlefield is crowded with well over one hundred and fifty screaming rioters racing in and out from all sides—women, children, and men wielding bludgeons and hurling rocks.

One of the men from the Pontiac, Roy Williams, levels his shotgun and begins firing. Another man, reported to be Amos Thompson, aims his shotgun and fires.[8] Pellets smash through the front passenger side window and rip through Jones, tearing pieces of flesh from his arms and face. More blasts from the shotguns are fired. Pellets imbed themselves into Dever's face and side.

Torn and bleeding, Jones exits the Blazer and empties a magazine from his M-16. Through gritted teeth he says, "Nobody is going to shoot me." For a moment, dozens of church members drop into the grass—and a moment later are back on their feet—unscathed! There is another burst from a shotgun—Jones falls, terribly wounded.

Rod Rothrock has seen one of the men fire. Still with one arm holding his twisting prisoner, the lawman draws his sidearm and fires one round. The man goes down into the grass. Rothrock never hears his own weapon fire—he looks at the weapon in disbelief and sees smoke. He watches the man who had dropped leap up—shotgun still in hand.

Gunfire Reports

The deputies' recollection of the amount and intensity of the gunfire varies greatly. Some recall almost every shot, while others recall only the gunfire that came their way. In the case of Rod Rothrock, he didn't hear his own weapon discharge. It is clear from all the stories that there were well over a hundred shots fired in the brief duration of the battle.[9]

Ray Thatcher remembers at least twenty shots that passed by his head while he was battling the mob. Captain Bert Goodman had five or six shots fired at him from close range, but he doesn't remember many other shots.[10]

Sergeant Buddy Hale recalls receiving small arms fire and after the Pontiac pulled up, there were at least four loud reports of shotguns being fired toward his position. At that point Hale distributed weapons from his own trunk, and gunfire became general.

It is interesting to note that Hale had a man charge toward him with a short shotgun aimed chest high. Hale was about to pull the trigger on him, but Deputy Rueben Leon knocked the assailant to the ground— saving the cult member's life. Sergeant Hale did not fire a shot that day.

Most of the deputies were amazed that they were receiving gunfire because of the proximity of the cult members that were physically engaging them in hand to hand combat.

Dever grabs the Blazer's radio mike—hoping for the staged DPS Officers to finally come to their aid. Dever yells, "Nine-nine-nine! Nine-nine-nine! Send the big guys, send all!" He drags Jones, torn and badly bleeding, into the bullet-riddled Blazer. He backs around the car that is blocking his exit and races for Highway Ninety-two. With the wind rushing through the shattered vehicle windows, Dever turns onto the highway—holding the steering wheel with one hand and trying to stem the flow of blood from a wound in Jones's chest with the other. Dever releases his pressure on the wound and periodically calls on his radio, "Need help! Nine-nine-nine. Call!"

Thatcher and Jark

When Deputy Ray Thatcher and his partner Dave Jark arrive on the scene, events that will eventually define the day begin to unfold. They drive to an open area at the far northeast quadrant of the compound. There is no such thing as an elevated position, but from where they park they have as good an observation point as can be found.

Thatcher is the SWAT team's designated sniper, and as such, his primary assignment is to remove, from a distance, any armed assailant attacking deputies anywhere in the area. Deputy Dave Jark is his backup.

No sooner do they exit their marked vehicle than they are challenged by twenty screaming women wielding rakes, hoes, and boards. Within an instant, Thatcher and Jark are involved in their own confrontations, each being battered and defending themselves against the blows as best they can. Thatcher uses the M-14 assault weapon defensively.

He holds it in front of him to deflect the blows from rakes and hoes. Many of the blows bash into his rifle stock, and just as many connect with his unprotected hands. The beatings continue for five or more minutes. Neither man returns a blow. They order the angry women to cease. None relents.

Jark finally yells to his partner, "Let's get out of here!"

Thatcher jumps on their car's hood. Jark leaps into the driver's seat and drives about two hundred feet further down Loaves and Fishes Road. But the women never stop. They continue to run with the car and pound the vehicle—and the exposed Thatcher—as it moves.

When Jark stops and Thatcher jumps off, the battle begins anew. Both officers are again fully engaged in overwhelming confrontations. Screaming women with boards, rakes, and hoes rain hits down on them. Thatcher ducks as a bullet flies past his head—and then another. Five or six rounds narrowly miss the deputy. Then another dozen or more bullets zip by his head. He is clearly being targeted. He is amazed that neither he nor his attackers are hit.

Jark is off to the right. He also has fended off Robert Luckett and his deadly numbchucks with a threat from his sidearm and is again being beaten by a group of screaming women. Thatcher, in the field still near Loaves and Fishes Road, is overwhelmed by at least seven angry women. He is being severely beaten—as he desperately fends off blows.

Ray Thatcher's hands are turning into mush. The stock of his M-14 is gouged and bent. The badge on his chest is a lump of twisted metal. He commands the attackers to "Back off!" Thatcher was born and raised in Texas. He has been taught to never hit a woman, but he is running out of options.

"Back off! Back off or you'll force me to fight back!"

A tall, substantial woman moves in and bashes him on his left shoulder. They have been warned. Thatcher's decision has been made. He returns her blow with equal force. He strikes her across the face with the stock of his weapon.

Lieutenant Homer Fletcher, involved in his own fight for life, sees it out of the corner of his eye. The woman Thatcher strikes lifts up off her feet and plops to the ground—incredibly—only to jump back up and continue her attack.

Thatcher's other assailants also continue the attack. The tall woman again is smashing away at him. He strikes her a second time. Again, she goes down, but leaps back up. From then on, the big deputy from Texas hits back when he is hit. But the women are still twenty and he is one.

Is Jark to the right fighting his own battle? Is he fighting back? Thatcher certainly can't tell. Every deputy in the field is focused on his own confrontation—they are barely aware of what is happening anywhere, with exception of the narrow scope of vision directly in front of them. Everything is moving with incredible speed, but time is extending for what seems an eternity.

But then, the deep bellow of shotgun blasts gets almost everybody's attention. To Thatcher's left, Dever and Jones are taking rounds. Thatcher sees a man fire shotgun blasts—shots tearing Jones apart and wounding Dever. Jark sees the shots as well.

As Dever drags his partner into the Blazer, Williams aims his shotgun. Jark draws his service revolver and squeezes off a round. Williams drops to the dirt before he can inflict any further harm to the already-wounded deputies. [11]

As Larry Dever speeds his severely injured partner Jones to the Sierra Vista Community Hospital, incensed women continue to beat Deputy Thatcher. He is now fighting back, but is overwhelmed. He starts to realize that he is being pushed to the east a step at a time—almost as if by plan. They continue to bash at him, herding him. He swings back with the butt of his rifle. Thatcher is taking much more than he is able to return. Bullets continue to whiz over his head from somewhere to the west and north.

Thatcher's first indication that things are somehow changing is when the blows begin to diminish. The women are backing off. Mission accomplished. Only a few are continuing to strike him—then none. Something is causing them to cease their frenzied attacks and it certainly isn't him fighting back.

To his right is movement—slow and smooth. It is William Thomas, Jr., walking at an easy pace, calm, with no discernible expression. It is now Field Marshal William Thomas, Jr.'s show and the women have backed off to give him room to operate.

Thatcher sees Thomas coming from the right. Thomas is determined—he is in no hurry. Thatcher sees the Winchester Ninety-four, thirty-thirty rifle hanging casually in his right hand, hammer back, ready to fire—only needing to be raised and the trigger pulled.

This is the same William Thomas, Jr., who Thatcher has talked with dozens of times. He is no stranger.

"Put the rifle down!" Thatcher yells at William Thomas, Jr., his worst fears bursting to the surface.

"Put the rifle down! Drop it now!"

Thatcher never stops yelling his orders as Thomas continues to walk in a slow arc from behind the deputy to a spot directly in front of him—no more than sixteen feet separate the two armed men. The Winchester still hangs limply in Thomas's hand, still cocked and ready.

"Drop it! Drop it now!"

William Thomas, Jr. slowly raises his weapon with a placid expression on his face. The deputy, his rifle still at his hip, never stops commanding, "Drop it! Drop it now!"

Thomas brings the rifle to his shoulder and takes dead aim at Deputy Thatcher.

The time for decisions and hesitation has ended. Thatcher knows he has already waited too long. Thatcher calls his final warning.

Then, with no other option, his Ruger Mini-fourteen at his waist—Deputy Thatcher fires four rounds into William Thomas, Jr.

Nearby, Sergeant Loyce Guthrie stops in her tracks and looks toward the gunshots. She sees William Thomas, Jr., sitting in the tall weeds in front of Thatcher. He falls back. Several women start for their fallen bishop. Then Deputy Guthrie sees the second man.

Aruguster Tate, William Thomas, Jr.'s father-in-law, walks from the side into Thatcher's view. Thatcher sees him bend down—but not to look at his son-in-law. Tate picks up the Winchester. Deputy Thatcher realizes—it's not over!

Again Thatcher yells, "Put it down! Drop the gun!" But that isn't what Tate has in mind. In a bizarre replay of the nightmare that has just played out, Tate gazes toward the deputy with the same placid expression of William Thomas, Jr. Time slows down—the cocked and ready Winchester Ninety-four is being raised.

Thatcher yells his commands—deputies all over the battlefield hear him. "Drop the gun!"

The rifle reaches Tate's shoulder and the commands stop. Thatcher, Mini-fourteen still at his hip, fires four rounds into the man's chest. He crumples—dying.

Two churchmen lay dead or dying in the field. Tate has fallen almost on top of William Thomas, Jr. CMHCC men and women drop to their knees wailing. Lieutenant Homer Fletcher sees a woman in a long dress slip the Winchester under her dress and disappear into the crowd. The weapon is never seen again.

Dave Jark hears the radio command to pull out and runs to Thatcher's position. "We're pulling out. Now!" They walk to their vehicle. There is no longer any need to run. The Shootout at Miracle Valley is over. As the deputies withdraw, bystander Urbane Leinendecker watches them. The man that started it all with his gift to A. A. Allen sees the final fruits of his charity.

Miracle Valley had become a powder keg, eagerly waiting, seeking a spark. Sheriff Judd's and every deputy's worst fear was that they might be forced into firing. They all hoped it would be peacefully resolved, but everyone feared the worst. The deputies endured beatings with pipes, rebar, rocks and two by fours. They were fired upon repeatedly during the melee. Ray Thatcher was badly beaten. The blows to his hands turned them into bloody swollen hams at the end of his arms.

Vince Madrid's forearms were shattered. Dave Jones and Larry Dever endured shotgun blasts. Homer Fletcher was knocked unconscious and then stabbed repeatedly with a broken bottle. Dave Jark was stabbed in the back with a knife.

Mild-mannered, soft spoken, and well-liked rookie Deputy Jeff Brown paid the ultimate price. Of the thirty-five deputies involved in the Shootout at Miracle Valley, twenty-five sustained serious injuries. Rick Tutor remembers Jeff as an "effective and smart law enforcement person. He wasn't overly aggressive and he was kind both to his fellow deputies and to the public." He concludes that, "Jeff Brown was a gentle person." [12]

Overwhelmed by numbers, deputies suffered shattered bones and vicious assaults as long as they could; for almost fifteen minutes of relentless combat, the deputies limited the use of deadly force. With the exception of Roy Williams (the man that shot Deputy Dave Jones and Sergeant. Larry Dever) no church member had been shot before Thatcher's confrontation. No deputy wanted to fire. Deputy Ray Thatcher, when he looked death in the eyes twice, fired the shots that brought the Shootout at Miracle Valley to a close.

Deputy Rick Tutor (right) discards his nightstick and grabs a pick handle to defend himself. Coming to his aid is Brad Geeck (with nightstick). The man wearing the cowboy hat (left) is Captain Bert Goodman. Photo courtesy of the Arizona Daily Star.

Deputy Rod Rothrock (right) fends off an attacker as more of Pastor Thomas' flock enter the fray. Sergeant Loyce Guthrie (far left with back to camera) and Deputies Gary Smith (second from left) and Vince Madrid form a defensive ring as two rock throwing church members rush toward them. Photo courtesy of the Arizona Daily Star.

Deputy Ray Thatcher retreats as one of a group of pursuing women (others not shown in this frame) hurls a large rock at him. Thatcher is being "pushed" to a location where he will have a deadly encounter with William Thomas Jr. and Arguster Tate. Photo courtesy of the Arizona Daily Star.

The deputies are being engulfed. Deputy facing the camera is Bill Townsend. Photo courtesy of the Arizona Daily Star.

Deputy Jeff Brown (left) faces four attackers. One woman is heaving a large rock as a second swings at the deputy with a pipe. Brown will meet more attackers in his ten minutes of hell—suffering injuries that will take his life. Photo courtesy of the Cochise County Sheriff's Department.

A wounded Sergeant Larry Dever exits his black Blazer moments after a shotgun blast blows through both the passenger window and the driver's window. Dave Jones is seated in the passenger seat. Jones will get out of the vehicle and be hit by another shotgun round. Photo courtesy of the Arizona Daily Star.

Lieutenant Craig Emanuel (right) tries to subdue an attacker. Behind him another deputy is about to be attacked by a church member (left). Photo courtesy of the Cochise County Sheriff's Department.

Seven or more women, armed with rocks, pipes and a baseball bat, force a deputy (far left) to retreat. Part of the tactics used by the CMHCC members was to use women to attack the deputies in close quarters. They thought the deputies wouldn't use their firearms against women. They were right. Photo courtesy of the Cochise County Sheriff's Department.

A woman races in to help five or six other women attack a deputy.
Notice one woman is swinging a long pipe. Photo courtesy of the
Cochise County Sheriff's Department.

Captain Bert Goodman (left) watches a church member flee with a shotgun.
Deputy Ray Thatcher has had his deadly encounter with William Thomas
Jr. and Arguster Tate. In moments, the Sheriff's men will receive orders to
withdraw to Highway 92. Photo courtesy of the Arizona Daily Star.

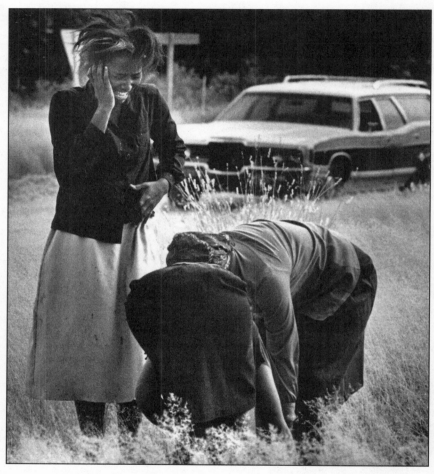

A member of the Christ Miracle Healing Center and Church grieves as two women try to lift the body of one of the two men killed in the shootout. Photo courtesy of the Arizona Daily Star.

A Planned Response

While the CMHCC members didn't engage the Cochise County Sheriff's deputies the morning of October 23, 1982, with a military-type strategy, there was a definite plan behind their tactics. Many of the church members had received training in weapons and combat. There was also a loose command structure. Much of this organization can be attributed to William Thomas's experience in the military. It is reported that groups of Pastor Thomas's followers would meet in front of their church and practice marching on a regular basis.

Previous tactics of church members had emphasized swarming and intimidating law officers. The Shootout at Miracle Valley escalated this tactic to include actual armed assaults. Swarms of women, men, and even children would keep the deputies divided while shooters on the perimeter would try to pick them off. [13] Finally, members of the Security Patrol would move in to confront the deputies.

It is reported that in response to Harold Hurtt's alleged call to Pastor Thomas, gunmen had been stationed in the buildings surrounding the field where the battle was to occur. An irony that played in favor of the deputies that day was the fatigue factor—church members were always operating in some state of sleep deprivation.

Many of the gunmen retired after spending a sleepless night waiting for Sheriff Judd's men to arrive. In the process they turned in most of their weapons. The weapons were secured in a locked room at the church. [14]

If Sheriff Judd's force had arrived an hour earlier, there probably would have been a massacre. Pastor Thomas's words to Harold Hurtt would have proven true: "If they come, none of them will leave this valley alive."

Endnotes

[1] Interview with Bert Goodman, February 23, 2006.

[2] Interview with Jim Self, August 23, 2008. (Sergeant Jim Self, Deputies Jim Hargrave, and James Allaire were among the first to arrive to aid Captain Goodman and Deputy Halloran.)

[3] Interview with Al Tomlinson, September 11, 2007.

[4] Interview with Bill Breen on August 27, 2008. (As an investigator for ACISA Breen had no authority to aid the deputies.)

[5] Interview with Rick Tutor, September 17, 2008.

[6] At the time of the writing of this book former Deputy Buddy Hale was preparing to undergo his sixth knee operation. The damage to legs and knees caused by George Gillespie ended Hale's career as a Cochise County Sheriff's deputy.

[7] Interview with Rick Tutor, September 17, 2008.

[8] Amos Thompson was the most heavily charged of the church members. He faced seven felony counts, including the attempted murder of Sgt. Larry Dever and Deputy Dave Jones. Sierra Vista Daily Herald February 8, 1983.

[9] The Arizona Republic, October 24, 1982.

[10] Interviews with Ray Thatcher and Bert Goodman, August 11, 2007.

[11] Neither the shot fired by Rothrock or by Jark wounded Roy Williams. Williams was wounded and paralyzed as a result of the shootout. However, when he died years later an autopsy found a .22 caliber slug in his back. He had apparently been shot accidentally by a church member during the fight.

[12] Interview with Rick Tutor, September 17, 2008.

[13] Interview with Bill Breen on August 27, 2008.

[14] Interview with Jim Self, August 23, 2008.

Chapter Twenty-five

A Trip to the Hospital

October 23, 1982—Later Morning

Upon their withdrawal from the bloody battlefield, Sheriff Judd and the deputies set up checkpoints going in and out of Miracle Valley. Sheriff Judd and his deputies stood at the entrance to the old A. A. Allen Bible College. They could hear singing in the CMHCC tabernacle directly across the highway. One of the Sheriff's first acts was to call the DPS and request that Sergeant Paul Larimer of the Cooperative Enforcement Unit be sent to take control of the battlefield and investigate the shooting.[1]

At the same time, the Sheriff's Office was receiving calls from terrified residents in Miracle Valley, requesting evacuation. Deputy Jim Self and others made countless forays into the valley immediately after the shootout and brought out residents.[2]

Even though injured during the battle, Sergeant Buddy Hale established a roadblock near the church's day-care center. Periodically, men would emerge from the structure waving guns, and then they would run back inside the building. Sergeant Hale instructed his men not to fire on them unless they were fired upon. From where Hale was stationed, he was one of the first to see the procession.

At first one and then a long line of police cars, their lights flashing, rolled south along Highway Ninety-two from Sierra Vista to reinforce the sheriff. The Highway Patrol was starting to arrive. Several other cars from Pima County also arrived—courtesy of Pima County Sheriff Clarence Dupnik. Dupnik's men were responding specifically to the 999 calls. (The nine-nine-nine code was an emergency request for any lawman hearing the call to come to the aid of their fellow lawmen.) The DPS began to set up roadblocks as the injured were beginning to exit Miracle Valley.

Where was the DPS?

The night before the shootout, the DPS ordered their District Nine Highway Patrol units to assemble at their headquarters in Sierra Vista. The support apparently promised to Sheriff Judd appeared to be in place the morning of the shootout. The problem was the support was never forthcoming. The DPS hierarchy—most likely Ralph Milstead—issued an order that under no circumstances were DPS Officers to become involved with the Miracle Valley operation or come to the aid of the Cochise County deputies unless authorized to do so. The ultimate responsibility for this failure of support must technically fall to Governor Bruce Babbitt. *Only* the governor had the authority to order the DPS to assist a county sheriff.[4] Sheriff Judd had asked for this support from the governor and to his dying day thought it would be provided if his deputies needed it. Apparently, the phone call from the governor to the DPS officers waiting in Sierra Vista never came.

In any case, the message that came down the chain of command was one of restraint. Apparently, Milstead's second in command told the local unit commander, DPS Lieutenant Jim Russell to "keep our people out of this."

The DPS (Highway Patrol) officers stood by their cars in the parking lot of the District Nine headquarters when the 999 calls from Miracle Valley started to crackle over Officer Kenneth Curfman's VHF radio. Curfman got in his car to respond. Lieutenant Russell asked Curfman, "What are you doing?"

Curfman replied, "Sir, they need help down there right now."

Russell replied, "We do not have the authority without being told by the Governor's office."

"Sir, I can not wait any longer. These guys need help and I'm going to help them," declared Curfman.

Curfman pulled out and headed for Miracle Valley, "knowing I had ruined my Highway Patrol career."[5] After a few minutes, other cars left the parking lot for Miracle Valley. The consequences for Curfman were as he predicted. He came under heavy pressure from his superiors for his violation of orders and eventually resigned.[6] Because of Curfman's decision to put principle over career, he forever won the respect and admiration of Sheriff Judd.

When asked to speculate on what may have motivated Bruce Babbitt's actions or inaction, a person prominently involved with the events laughed, "You got to understand, Bruce Babbitt isn't like us. He breathes bottled air and we get to breathe what's left over."

Bruce Babbitt Calls

Shortly after the shootout, Sheriff Judd received a phone call from Governor Bruce Babbitt—the man who apparently failed to give DPS Director Milstead the authority to send the Highway Patrol into Miracle Valley to support the Cochise County Sheriff's Department. (See Where was the DPS?) Babbitt's short conversation with Judd ends with the assurance, "Don't worry about it. We're in this together."

The next thing Jimmy Judd sees are thirty-five FBI agents descending on Miracle Valley. Judd asks their head man, "who called you to come down here?" He replies,"Bruce Babbitt." Judd's response is, "Like Hell, we're in this together."[3]

Faith Healing

The bulk of the deputies had set up operations in the parking lot of Allen's old Bible college. A weary Deputy Ray Thatcher turned his weapon over to a superior. Sheriff Judd was still at the highway across from the cult's church.

The black 1979 Lincoln and another car came south on Healing Way and turned onto Highway Ninety-two. Sheriff Jimmy Judd stepped onto the highway with several deputies. The car stopped, and the front-passenger window rolled down. Jimmy Judd was staring into the face of Pastor Thomas. The driver exited and accompanied a deputy to the trunk. Other deputies inspected the second car.

Jimmy glanced in at the back seat. The bodies of Aruguster Tate and William Thomas, Jr. were sprawled on the seat. Sheriff Judd expressed his condolences to Pastor Thomas.

She replied, "You killed my son."

He answered, "No ma'am, you killed your son."[7]

The window rolled up. The deputy removed some weapons from the trunk, and Sheriff Judd allowed the grieving mother to take her son and Aruguster Tate to the hospital in Sierra Vista. Pastor Thomas, who claimed she had resurrected Steven Lindsey and permitted four or five children to die because of her belief in faith healing, now wanted a hospital to perform a miracle.

Unarmed

When Sergeant Dever arrived at the Sierra Vista hospital, he was unarmed by a city policeman, as was typical police policy after an incident involving a gun. However, the policeman left, and members of the Church began arriving to have their injuries treated.

Sergeant Larry Dever shortly after the gunfight. Dever was wounded in the side and face. Photo courtesy of the Arizona Daily Star.

Dever found himself in the midst of CMHCC members that were seeking a non-faith-healing treatment. Realizing that just a half an hour earlier he had been fighting these people, he called the Sierra Vista Substation for backup.

Despite his unease, the battle was over—like someone had flipped a switch. The church members ignored him.[8]

Deputy Rick Tutor remembers the hospital scene as one of chaos. Both deputies and church members were being treated. "It was something like you would see on *MASH*," noted Tutor. The deputy looked out the door of the treatment room as his broken fingers were being attended to. He saw two bodies in the hall on gurneys, covered by sheets—William Thomas, Jr. and Arguster Tate.[9]

A Good Deed Undone

In one of those odd twists of fate that Arizona seems so blessed or cursed with, Urbane Leinendecker witnessed the Shootout at Miracle Valley. Leinendecker, who had given A. A. Allen the land on which to build his Bible college, was house sitting in Miracle Valley when the shootout started. Leinendecker went outside and watched. He saw Arguster Tate raise the rifle toward Deputy Thatcher and watched the deputy shoot him. It is not known if God spoke to Leinendecker again, but he fled the scene on his bicycle to the Bible college across the highway.

Get the Deputy

As noted, Sergeant Larimer's unit was assigned to investigate the shooting that occurred in Miracle Valley. He strongly believes that the arrival of the FBI agents was a "get the deputy (Ray Thatcher) event." Larimer had written the Tucson FBI office a year earlier recommending that they needed to investigate Pastor Frances Thomas and her sect. They ignored him.[10]

Like many of his contemporaries, Larimer believes the FBI had a political agenda. When he met with the agents he noted his disdain for them, but cooperated. Larimer's investigation exonerated Deputy Ray Thatcher of any wrongdoing in the shooting of William Thomas, Jr. and Arguster Tate.

Deputy Rick Tutor also wondered about the FBI's intentions when they read him his Miranda Rights. Despite this, he continued to answer all their questions.[11]

As noted, Larimer's report found that Deputy Ray Thatcher acted in self-defense when he shot William Thomas, Jr. and Arguster Tate.[12] According to more than one account, after Larimer submitted his report, it was returned to him. Larimer was told it wasn't correct. He submitted the same report a second time and was told if he didn't reconsider it, he would never see lieutenant. Larimer is said to have responded that he would just have to skip lieutenant and become captain. Larimer was considered a hero by Jimmy Judd, who hired him after he left the DPS.

On the same day the shootout occurred, Leinendecker was interviewed. "It almost made me vomit that I didn't have a pistol in my hand," Leinendecker remarked. "I'm a dead shot."[13]

Eyewitness Urbane Leinendecker gives reporters his account of the gun battle that claimed two lives. Photo courtesy of the Herald Dispatch and Bisbee Review.

Endnotes

[1] Interview with Paul Larimer, September 4, 2008.

[2] Interview with Jim Self, August 23, 2008.

[3] The Arizona Republic, October 25, 1987.

[4] Interview with Kenneth Curfman, September 17, 2008.

[5] Interview with Kenneth Curfman, September 17, 2008.

[6] At a party for Jimmy Judd's retirement as justice of the peace for Benson, Kenneth Curfman rose and made a moving speech. He told Jimmy that "I followed you into hell once and I would do it again."

[7] Interview with Virgil Judd, August 12, 2008.

[8] Interview with Larry Dever, September 11, 2007.

[9] Interview with Rick Tutor, September 17, 2008.

[10] Interview with Paul Larimer, September 4, 2008.

[11] Interview with Rick Tutor, September 17, 2008.

[12] In an interview with Dr. R. C. Froede on September 18, 2008, the nationally renowned medical examiner (who had performed the autopsies on William Thomas, Jr. and Arguster Tate) confirmed the autopsies were consistent with Deputy Thatcher's statements and to eye witness accounts. Unlike some sensational news broadcasts of that time, Dr. Froede confirmed, "There were no back to front wounds."

[13] The Arizona Republic, October 25, 1987.

Chapter Twenty-six

The Firestorm

Jesse Jackson

The Shootout at Miracle Valley created a worldwide news event. It made headlines as far away as Bangkok, Thailand.

But in the United States, it made more than headlines. It created a national furor and outrage. Many ministers and churches offered their support, both moral and physical, to Pastor Thomas and members of her flock. Many members of the church took temporary shelter in homes and churches in the Tucson area. Many politicians, statewide and nationwide, were so busy pointing fingers of blame at the sheriff that they overlooked the fact that they were indulging in the same stereotyping and bigotry they were accusing Jimmy Judd of committing.

Pastor Thomas's civil rights suit against Cochise County and the sheriff was amended to include the alleged "unlawful deaths of William Thomas, Jr. and Aruguster Tate." In such a charged environment, and considering his close relationship with Governor Bruce Babbitt, the Reverend Jesse Jackson could not resist the need to conduct a fact-finding mission to Miracle Valley.

It has been asserted Governor Babbitt wanted Jackson's influence to gain minority support for his presidential ambitions. The Shootout at Miracle Valley had not contributed to the governor's prospects. At the same time, perhaps Jesse Jackson had his own, unannounced agenda. Jackson announced his bid for the presidency in 1983.

The Public Visit

"A confrontation for the sole purpose of the assassination of William Thomas, Jr."

—Attributed to Reverend Jesse Jackson

A Misunderstood Man and Bad Press

Sheriff Judd was underestimated by his foes more than once. They also misjudged his intentions and imposed on him their own, often-incorrect judgments. A report issued for Cochise County, which studied the County's position and prospects in the looming Civil Rights Action brought against them by Pastor Thomas, touched upon this.

The report mentions the "constant media attack during the last twelve months that has been unequaled since the Arizona Land fraud scandals of the early 1970s. Radio talk shows, editorials, TV specials, and gallons of ink—all bad have been present."

The report goes on to describe most of this attitude as a result of "white men's guilt" as opposed to facts or reality.

"In Cochise County cowboy boots and Stetsons are the uniform of the day. In Tucson and Phoenix it means redneck" the report continued. The report recommended despite this perception "that the County should not settle the case out of court." It also recommended that Sheriff Judd not wear his Stetson and cowboy boots to the trial.[1]

In addition, there was the personal toll on Jimmy Judd. Edna Judd waited for her husband to come home after the shootout. In the early morning before sunrise, she heard a noise outside their home. She went to investigate and found Jimmy Judd leaning against the side of the house weeping. She comforted him, telling him that the deceased had done bad things. The sheriff responded, "Yes, but they were someone's sons and someone's fathers."[2]

Operation PUSH (People United to Save Humanity) leader, Jesse Jackson, in the company of some Chicago ministers, went to Miracle Valley and toured the community. The Jackson entourage declined to have Cochise County Sheriff deputies escort them into Miracle Valley. Instead Jackson, his staff and their three cars were accompanied by the three DPS Highway Patrolmen, including Officer Kenneth Curfman. Jackson and his body guards emphasized that Curfman and the two other officers were to "stay very close." They also wanted a plan for a quick extraction from Miracle Valley if it was needed.[3] They first met with leaders of the church who had not gone to Chicago.

At a press conference in Miracle Valley, Jackson said he "was

Operation PUSH leader Jesse Jackson conducts a "fact finding" trip to Miracle Valley. Jackson stands in the field where William Thomas Jr. and Arguster Tate were shot. He was critical of the Cochise County Sheriff's Office. Photo courtesy of the Arizona Daily Star.

[there] representing ministers from around the United States that had a grave concern about what [had] been happening [there] for about a two year period." Jackson further stated that Governor Babbitt likewise shared their concern. He added, "And all of us have a commitment to make sure to the extent possible there is no more bloodshed and no more violence."

He further told about meeting with Reverend Thomas, her family, and members of the church in Chicago. "Mr. William Thomas and Aruguster Tate were funeralized [sic] at our Chicago [Operation PUSH] headquarters," Jackson said.[4]

A Chicago Funeral

The four-hour funeral of William Thomas, Jr. and Arguster Tate had many speakers. Among them was Reverend Willie Barrow, special assistant to Reverend Jesse Jackson. She turned the attendees' attention back to the shootout.

Reading from an Operation Push statement, she declared, "The slaying of Bishop Thomas and Brother Arguster Tate represents one of the greatest tragedies of our time. The Miracle Valley incidents, or more appropriately 'murders,' are a travesty. Our organization accordingly has called for a full-scale investigation into this heinous crime."

She added that she could see that William Thomas, Jr. and Arguster Tate were already talking with the late Dr. Martin Luther King, Jr., and the saints in paradise.[5]

In a revealing statement, Jackson said he was surprised to learn of the number of Latino and white people in the community—and of their interpersonal relationships with the members of Mrs. Thomas's flock.

He declared, "All of you that are living here are victims of what happened on the twenty-third." He then honed his message, complaining that terrorism in "Northern Ireland is met with rubber bullets and not M-16's. Even the American soldiers that are in Lebanon today as peacekeepers do not put clips in their M-16's."[6]

Taking a final swipe at the Cochise County Sheriff's Department, Jackson questioned the legality of the use of M-16's by law officers. He noted the number of bullet holes in the homes in Miracle Valley as a sign of excessive force—not realizing almost all of them were the result of Pastor Thomas's followers.

After residents of Miracle Valley started explaining to Jackson the difficulties they had faced because of the cult, and the help they had offered to individual church members, Jackson tried to conclude the meeting. Seventy-five year old May Belle Taylor (black and a former follower of A. A. Allen) confronted Jackson about the real motives and actions of Pastor Thomas. Jackson made a hurried exit.[7] After visiting Miracle Valley for less than an hour, Jackson left and dismissed his Highway Patrol escort.

Jesse Jackson's next stop after leaving Miracle Valley was a visit to the Cochise County Sheriff's sub station in Sierra Vista. Jackson, a couple of aides, Lieutenant Gene Kellogg (of the Sheriff's office), DPS Sergeant Paul Larimer, and several other law enforcement people met in the basement of the substation. During Jackson's fact gathering effort he produced a denim shirt he said he had picked up from the field where William Thomas, Jr. and Arguster Tate were shot. Jackson indicated he thought it was evidence.

Larimer, who was in charge of investigating the shooting scene, requested the shirt from Jackson. Jackson responded that he was not going to give it to the investigator. Sergeant Larimer told Jackson, "You can either give me the shirt or I'll arrest you and take it." Jackson gave him the shirt.[8]

The Secret Meeting

Another meeting Jackson had was unpublicized—secret. Even today, there is little known of the meeting. On a deserted road in Cochise County, Jesse Jackson and his entourage parked their limousines on the gravel shoulder. A couple of minutes later, Sheriff Jimmy Judd pulled up behind the three cars and exited his vehicle. He passed a car and a door opened.

The smiling face of Jackson greeted Judd. The sheriff climbed into the car and the two men talked. Jackson appeared "sincere and interested" in Jimmy's side of the story. The sheriff explained how the CMHCC impacted Cochise County and how he and his men had bent over backward to avoid conflict and violence—to the point of being accused of enforcing the law unequally. He emphasized how many times violence had been avoided by the restraint of his men.

Jackson listened and shook his head affirmatively several times. Jackson told Judd, "I can see you were doing what was right." That night, Jimmy told his wife, "that he [Jackson] was a nice fellow—fair." He wondered why so many people disliked Jackson.

"That son of a bitch," was the sheriff's comment when he saw a televised interview with Jackson accusing the sheriff's department of the use of excessive force.[9]

Disappearing Act

Pastor Thomas and many of her followers went to Chicago for the funeral of Aruguster Tate and William Thomas, Jr.[10] There were still some church members in Miracle Valley—they attended church, tended to their animals and pets, went to work, and tried to carry on with their lives.

Then, one day they left en masse. Suddenly, Pastor Thomas's flock got into their cars and dozens of vehicles poured out of Miracle Valley. The caravan rolled east. They left almost everything behind. Meals were left on tables, water in sinks, and pets in the yard. It was time to go—and as if on command they left unannounced—just as they had arrived.

Legal Injustice

The wheels of justice moved slowly. There were approximately twenty-one church members charged with approximately 70 felony counts.[11] Amos Thompson was accused of shooting Deputy Jones and Sergeant Dever. Ricky Lamar, the man that had apparently crushed the chest of Jeff Brown, also waited for his day in court.

The trials never happened. The legal proceedings were bankrupting Cochise County. In 1983, a court ordered that Cochise County would have to pay the legal fees of the defendants who assaulted the sheriff's men. In 1983, only Pima and Pinal County received money from the state for public defenders. Cochise County didn't have the money to continue the search for justice.

When Cochise County refused to pay for the defendants' legal costs and the cost of a possible change of venue, a higher court dismissed the cases. On February 22, 1984, the charges were thrown out permanently. The men and women that attacked the law officers went free. They got away with murder!

Another legal proceeding went more favorably for Cochise County. After a long investigation, the United States Justice Department found no wrongdoing on the part of the Cochise County Sheriff's Department, Sheriff Jimmy Judd or Deputy Ray Thatcher. The federal grand jury civil rights investigation into the deaths of William Thomas, Jr. and Arguster Tate was closed on September 6, 1984.

A final court preceding that never took place rocked Sheriff Judd and his deputies. They were preparing to defend themselves against the civil rights action brought by Pastor Thomas—in fact, they were looking forward to telling their story.

Cochise County—still teetering on the brink of bankruptcy—against the advice of their counsel, settled the lawsuit out of court.[12] Some lawmen were arriving at court for the first day of proceedings, when they were told of the settlement. The amount paid to Mrs. Thomas has never been officially disclosed. Back in Chicago, however, it was said that some of the pastor's flock were not happy because she was not sharing her windfall.[13] On the other hand, there may not have been all that much to share. One source indicated that the settlement amounted to five hundred thousand dollars.[14] Of this amount, it is reported that all but fifty thousand dollars went to Thomas's lawyers. In addition, it was said that some of the lawyers were suing her for the balance.

Cochise County Supervisor Judy Gignac said, "I certainly didn't want to pay them (the church members) for the privilege of harassing us and beating up our deputies. Gignac was also upset that the true story of Miracle Valley might not ever be told. [15]

A Parting Shot

Sheriff Jimmy Judd's personal odyssey into hell did not end on October 23, 1982. Approximately a month after the Shootout at Miracle Valley, Judd was driving west on I-10 towards Tucson. He was going to pick up his son Virgil, who had just completed a two-year church mission to Brazil.[16] Judd was running late. His wife Edna, sons Morgan and Tye and daughters Margo and Lyle had gone ahead of him.

On the day of the attempted assassination, Sheriff Judd's family went the Tucson airport ahead of him. (Back row, left to right) Morgan, Tye and Virgil. (Front row, left to right) Lyle and Margo. Virgil was returning from Brazil.

Sheriff Judd's vehicle was traveling at sixty-five miles per hour as it passed Marsh Station. An impatient Judd pushed the vehicle up to seventy miles per hour when a rifle shot slammed through the passenger window directly behind him. It missed his head by a foot. Judd floored the accelerator. The Sheriff escaped death, but he and his family lived with the knowledge that they were not safe.

This was not a sloppy assassination attempt. It was not a man emerging from the side of the road with a shotgun or someone thinking they were going to kill the

Sheriff with a crude bomb. The shooter had laid in wait with a high power rifle. According to Judd, it was at least a hundred yard shot. The perpetrator had known Judd would be traveling the Interstate at that time because the news of Virgil's arrival at the Tucson Airport had been in all the local papers. All the shooter had to do was to be patient. It was clear, the shooter was a professional. The rumors of a "hit" being put out on Sheriff Judd were true.

The question of who hired the "hit man" is more intriguing. Someone had the connections and sophistication to find and pay a true professional. Though the identity of the shooter is unknown, the identity of the person who hired him is less ambiguous. Jimmy Judd was sure he knew who hired the "hit man." Today, there are several people who know who this individual is. However, until there is additional collaborative evidence the person will go unnamed.[17]

Jimmy Judd and his wife Edna.

A Chance Meeting

In February, 1990, a new director was appointed to the Arizona Department of Public Safety. Ralph Milstead stepped down from his post and into retirement after overseeing that department during some of its most turbulent years. In 1991, Milstead was visiting Bisbee when he ran into Sheriff Jimmy Judd and his wife, Edna. Milstead had been critical of Judd's management of the Miracle Valley affair. "He (Milstead) came over to me and said, 'I guess you'd like to punch me in the mouth.' I said, 'Yeah.' He apologized to me. It takes a big man to do that. Now we get along great."[18]

In addition, Milstead said he should have given support to Judd on the day of the shootout. The two men shook hands and went their separate ways. Although Judd accepted Milstead's apology and they got along okay, the Sheriff never again gave him his trust.[19]

After the Dust Settled

Sheriff Jimmy Judd was re-elected Sheriff of Cochise County by a large majority. He served a total of four terms running from 1976 through 1992. After leaving the sheriff's department, Judd returned to the position of Benson justice of the peace. He passed away at the age of seventy-two.

Sergeant Larry Dever ran for the position of Cochise County Sheriff in 1996. His ambition is to be re-elected to a fourth term like the man he served under, Sheriff Judd.

Captain Bert Goodman began his career with the Cochise County Sheriff's Department in January of 1961. He waited until all of the outstanding legal issues with Miracle Valley were settled and retired in October of 1984. He raises cattle on his ranch.

Rod Rothrock is currently the Chief Deputy of Cochise County.

Vince Madrid never completely recovered from his wounds, but at the time of the writing of this book, was working for a private security company in Afghanistan.

Pastor Frances Thomas returned to Chicago to live in relative obscurity.

Governor Bruce Babbitt never became president. He still serves on conservation committees and is an advocate for environmental causes. Sheriff Jimmy Judd never forgave what he considered was Bruce Babbitt's betrayal of the Cochise County Deputies.[20]

Former Phoenix Police Captain Harold Hurtt, the "governor's mediator," became the Chief of Police for Houston, Texas.

Bill Townsend is currently an Evidence Technician for the Department of Justice Drug Enforcement Administration.

Lora Triplett, who resisted being rescued by Deputy Bill Townsend, became a nurse in Chicago. In 1990, she called Townsend and thanked him for his bravery and apologized to him for her actions at that time.[21]

Rick Tutor paused when he was asked if he had any final thoughts on those turbulent years. He quietly concluded, "I loved my career with the Cochise County Sheriff's Department. I have no regrets."[22]

Twenty-seven years after the shootout at Miracle Valley retired Captain Bert Goodman (left), Cochise County Sheriff Larry Dever (center), and Retired Deputy Ray Thatcher (right) return to the scene of the melee to recall the events that occurred. Photo by William Daniel.

Retired Captain Bert Goodman uses a stick to describe how a man waved a long pipe at him at the beginning of the shootout. Behind him is a part of the field where much of the fight occurred. Photo by William Daniel.

Five years after the Shootout at Miracle Valley, an article appeared in The Arizona Republic. It was a candid interview with Julius "Gus" Gillespie. Gillespie had always considered himself the Pastor's "left hand man." He was the first member of the congregation to talk about the incident. He was no longer the loyal follower of Frances Thomas.

According to Gillespie, the "troubles" in Miracle Valley could have been avoided. He blamed the conflicts on the ambition, despotism and the prejudice of Frances Thomas. The main problem was that she "had a prejudice against whites." The one time firebrand for the CMHCC added, "The only thing I hate is the best years of my life are past...all I have to look back on is heartache."[23]

Ray Thatcher, the man who brought the October 23, 1982, battle to a close, still lives with the burden of what occurred: "It's something you can never take back." He tells of people giving him thumbs up and telling him "good job." Thatcher would smile back thinly, but they didn't understand.

Long after the shooting, Thatcher tells of hearing people say they "wish they could shoot somebody." A sad-eyed Thatcher says, "no you don't ...you don't ever want to do that." He adds that he often saw and talked with William Thomas, Jr.—he knew him. Though he still regrets the shooting, Thatcher realizes that if he had not defended himself, he would be dead. Looking away, Thatcher "hopes the shooting saved lives" by bringing the conflict to an end.

Endnotes

[1] Sacks, Status Report CIV 82-343 TUC ACM.

[2] Interview with Edna Judd, August 23, 2008.

[3] Interview with Kenneth Curfman, September 17, 2008.

[4] From Jackson meeting with Miracle Valley residents, November 11, 1982.

[5] Tucson Citizen, November 5, 1983.

[6] Exactly one year to the day after the Shootout at Miracle Valley tragedy struck the American Peace Keepers in Lebanon. On October 23rd, 1983 the Marine Barracks in Beirut were bombed. Two hundred and twenty marines were killed as were an additional twenty-one other servicemen.

[7] It is interesting to note that one resident in a sworn statement remarked immediately after the battle, he overheard a man (later identified as Pastor Thomas's brother) tell Thomas that he kept shooting at the deputies, but missing his targets.

[8] Interview with Paul Larimer, September 4, 2008.

[9] Told by Sheriff Judd to his close friend Larry Dempster and also related by members of the Judd family.

[10] Sacks, Status Report CIV 82-343 TUC ACM.

[11] Herald Dispatch and Bisbee Review, May 29, 1983.

[12] Sacks, Status Report CIV 82-343 TUC ACM.

[13] Lora Triplett per 1990 phone conversation with Deputy Bill Townsend.

[14] The Arizona Daily Star, January 5, 1988.

[15] The Arizona Daily Star, January 5, 1988.

[16] Interview with Virgil Judd, August 12, 2008. (It is interesting to note that Virgil Judd was in Rio de Janeiro at the time of the Shootout at Miracle Valley. He was preparing to return home after a two year church mission. He learned about the shootout by seeing the front cover of Brazil's equivalent of Time Magazine on a newsstand. The event was truly worldwide news.)

[17] Sources unnamed for their own protection.

[18] The Arizona Republic, October 25, 1987.

[19] Interview with Edna Judd, August 23, 2008.

[20] Interview with Edna Judd, August 23, 2008.

[21] Lora Triplett per 1990 phone conversation with Deputy Bill Townsend.

[22] Interview with Rick Tutor, September 17, 2008.

[23] "Ex-aide blames tragedy on church leader, not sheriff", The Arizona Republic, October 25, 1987.

Epilogue

Physical Similarities

The Gunfight at the OK Corral and the Shootout at Miracle Valley had remarkable similarities. Among them are the numbers of fatalities and the confined space in which both encounters took place.

Three men died in the Gunfight at the OK Corral (Frank McLaury, Tom McLaury, and Billy Clanton) and three men died as a result of the Shootout at Miracle Valley (Deputy Jeff Brown, William Thomas, Jr. and Arguster Tate).[1]

One of the most striking similarities of the two gunfights is the incredibly small space in which they took place. If one has ever visited the OK Corral site, they would be immediately struck that within the confines of an alley-like area were two horses and eight men. It is remarkable that only three men died in the brief gunfight.

Likewise, the Shootout at Miracle Valley occurred in a small field (bisected by a dirt road) and surrounded by a few buildings and trees. In that area over two hundred church members and thirty-five deputies waged an all-out fight. The possibility of a blood bath occurring was staggering.

Complex Issues

There were complex issues that lead up to both deadly encounters. The issues were political, economic and human; they were conflicts over control. The causes are still debated today; people still take sides and argue with passion about both events.

Also, people who have studied the fabled gunfight between the Earps with their friend Doc Holiday against the Clantons and McLaurys understand that the aftermath was no less complicated.

Our version of what happened on Oct 26, 1881 is often filtered by Wyatt Earp's book about the incident—since he outlived his contemporaries.

A little over one hundred years later, the Shootout at Miracle Valley leaves behind the same complex web of human emotions, ambition, and issues. The deputies that lived through the shootout on October 23, 1982, were forever impacted and changed by their ten to fifteen minutes in hell.

The Great Divide

The Shootout at Miracle Valley differs from the Gunfight at the OK Corral because of its deeply religious and racial components. These twin characteristics have made it a more painful and charged affair. The Shootout at Miracle Valley will never be romanticized, as is the Shootout at the OK Corral. Even though the deserted battlefield is little changed from the day of the shootout, it is doubtful thousands will ever trek to the site.

America still faces the issues that generated the Shootout at Miracle Valley. Radical ministers will rise again—preaching hate. The lesson is clear: racism, bolstered by religious fanaticism—no matter how it is disguised—will continue to spring forth until it and its practitioners are confronted and disavowed. Pastor Thomas was not the first hate-mongering preacher from Chicago, and she will not be the last.

Sheriff Jimmy Judd and the Cochise County Sheriff's deputies were not the first and will not be the last to raise their exercise of restraint to heroic levels. Perhaps their story is remarkable because it doesn't fit the stereotypes that our society so easily uses to define our racial conflicts.

And finally, beyond all hate, all restraint—beyond all pettiness and heroism—stands the true miracle of the Shootout at Miracle Valley. Whether by a sublime series of accidents or divine intervention, a blood bath did not occur. There was no Waco or Jonestown. There was only the *Miracle* at Miracle Valley.

Endnotes

[1] Roy Williams, who fired shotgun blasts that may have injured Sgt. Larry Dever and Deputy Dave Jones, was also shot during the battle. He was paralyzed and returned to Chicago. Several years later he died. Doctors attributed his death to complications resulting from his gunshot wound. It is reported that the bullet that was lodged in his back was from a .22 caliber weapon. He was shot by another CMHCC member during the shootout.

Acknowledgments

THIS BOOK IS THE result of a cooperative effort of persons who believed in the project and would not allow the Shootout at Miracle Valley to disappear into historical oblivion. Jimmy Judd's wish that the true story of Miracle Valley be told would have gone unfulfilled had it not been for the tenacity of his longtime friend, Larry Dempster. Likewise, without the Judd family's wholehearted support and dedication, this story would not have been written.

The deputies that were involved in the events leading up to and during the actual shootout were asked to relive painful memories. Their heroic efforts are chronicled within these pages. Among these men are Bert Goodman, Larry Dever, Ray Thatcher, Rod Rothrock, Buddy Hale, Bill Townsend, Al Tomlinson, Homer Fletcher, Jim Self, Vince Madrid, Don Barnett, Rick Tutor, and Frank Martinez. By necessity, many other brave officers and deputies go unmentioned but their courageous behavior on that day is not forgotten.

In addition, Bill Breen (a former investigator and analyst for ACISA) was extremely helpful as was retired CPE Lieutenant Paul Larimer, and Bart Goodwin (a former agent for the DPS Criminal Investigation Bureau). Thanks also to medical examiner Dr. R. C. Froede, former DPS Officer Kenneth Curfman and retired ATF Agent Hank Murray.

The recollections of the former Palominas School Superintendent Gene Brust were also invaluable in telling this story. The efforts of G. G. Robbins, who conducted many early interviews, also contributed to the process of bringing this story to life. Thanks also to Arizona film legend Robert Shelton, who brought me to the attention of Larry Dempster.

And finally, the support and keen eye for detail of Betsy Daniel should be noted. Her editing skills are as always indispensable. Her belief in me has never wavered.

References

THE SHOOTOUT AT MIRACLE Valley is the result of sifting through thousands of pages of newspaper articles, depositions, official and unofficial records, and dozens of interviews. The facts included in this book come from both public and private sources. While many sources of information in this book are footnoted, others go uncredited.

The documentation presented is a small account of the vast quantity of materials made available. For every incident related in this book, there are many other occurrences of the same nature that by necessity go untold.

As time moves on, the living sources of information are lost. Sheriff Jimmy Judd passed on before he was able to read this book, but his testimony is everywhere in its pages. Likewise, County Attorney Beverly Jenny is no longer with us.

This writer has had the opportunity to review an array of material that is staggering, both in its volume and breadth of content. It is doubtful this collection of material and resources will again be available to a single individual.

About the Author

WILLIAM R. DANIEL WAS born and raised in the Midwest. He helped pay for his college education by working as an investigator for a nationally known detective agency. Daniel has a journalism background and covered several Presidential elections. As an award winning photographer his pictures have appeared in Time Magazine, the New York Times, the Los Angeles Times and other prominent publications worldwide. He covered the Contra-Sandinista war and traveled extensively in Honduras and Nicaragua.

For fifteen years William and his wife Betsy owned a media company that serviced Fortune 500 companies. The company produced video, documentation and software solutions.

Daniel is a screenwriter and resides in Tucson, Arizona. *Shootout at Miracle Valley* is his first book.